WITHDRAWN

UNDERSTANDING
BERNARD MALAMUD

Understanding Contemporary American Literature

Matthew J. Bruccoli, *Editor*

UNDERSTANDING
Bernard
MALAMUD

BY JEFFREY HELTERMAN

UNIVERSITY OF SOUTH CAROLINA PRESS

Cover Photograph of Bernard Malamud
by Layle Silbert

Published in Columbia, South Carolina, by the University of South Carolina Press

Manufactured in the United States of America

Library of Congress Cataloging-in-Publication Data

Helterman, Jeffrey.
  Understanding Bernard Malamud.

  (Understanding contemporary American literature)
  Bibliography: p.
  Includes index.
  1. Malamud, Bernard—Criticism and interpretation.
I. Title.   II. Series.
PS3563.A4Z67   1985   813'.54   85-16413
ISBN 0-87249-470-5 (pbk.)
ISBN 0-87249-469-1

CONTENTS

EDITOR'S PREFACE

Understanding Contemporary American Literature has been planned as a series of guides or companions for students as well as good nonacademic readers. The editor and publisher perceive a need for these volumes because much of the influential contemporary literature makes special demands. Uninitiated readers encounter difficulty in approaching works that depart from the traditional forms and techniques of prose and poetry. Literature relies on conventions, but the conventions keep evolving; new writers form their own conventions—which in time may become familiar. Put simply, *UCAL* provides instruction in how to read certain contemporary writers—identifying and explicating their material, themes, use of language, point of view, structures, symbolism, and responses to experience.

The word *understanding* in the series title was deliberately chosen. Many willing readers lack an adequate understanding of how contemporary literature works; that is, what the author is attempting to express and the means by which it is conveyed. Although the level of criticism and analysis in the series has been aimed at a level of general accessibility, these introductory volumes are meant to be applied in conjunction with the works they cover. Thus they do not provide a substitute for the works and authors they introduce, but rather prepare the reader for more profitable literary experiences.

M.J.B.

UNDERSTANDING
BERNARD MALAMUD

CHAPTER ONE

Understanding Bernard Malamud

Career

Bernard Malamud grew up in a world not unlike that of his second novel, *The Assistant*. He was born in Brooklyn in 1914 and spent many hours of his youth behind the counter of a small grocery store run by his parents, immigrants like the Bobers of the novel. He graduated from Erasmus Hall High School in the middle of the Depression, whose hard economic times are reflected in much of his early fiction. Malamud went on to the City College of New York where he received a BA in 1936. Six years later he earned a master's degree in English from Columbia University. Malamud began writing stories at this time while he taught night classes, first at Erasmus and then at Harlem High School. In 1949, he joined the faculty of Oregon State University where he remained for a dozen years. He then moved to Bennington College where he still teaches on a part-time basis.

Malamud began his career as the American heir to the sophisticated tellers of Yiddish folktales like I. B. Singer and Isaac Babel. He had already published *The Natural* (1952), a comic overlay of the Grail romance on a baseball story, and a

UNDERSTANDING BERNARD MALAMUD

much more mature work, *The Assistant* (1958), when, in 1959, he won the National Book Award for a luminescent collection of short stories, *The Magic Barrel*. As one responds to the consistently mystical quality of these portraits of man's humanity and inhumanity to man, it is easy to appreciate the anticipation that swept through editors of *Commentary* when a new Malamud piece arrived. They knew they would find tales of small men whose little actions meant the difference between lamenting and celebrating the fate of mankind. Malamud's characters, often haunted by the Holocaust, look clumsily for a little grace in their lives. Some find it, many don't, but always they tell us the truth about their frailty and our own. Malamud says of his own heroes, "A Malamud character is someone who fears his fate, is caught up in it, yet manages to outrun it. He's the subject and object of laughter and pity."[1] The prolific period from 1958 to 1966 established Malamud as one of the foremost writers of moral fiction in America. In addition to *The Assistant* and *The Magic Barrel*, Malamud published *A New Life* (1961), a somewhat autobiographical academic novel based on his twelve years of teaching at Oregon State University; *Idiots First* (1963), a second collection of short stories more broad-ranging in subject matter than the first; and his masterpiece, *The Fixer* (1966), for which he won his second National Book Award. In his celebration of the moral courage of fools and idiots, Malamud's morality begins to take on a New Testament look and, paradoxically, a character may become more Christlike as he becomes more Jewish. Most of this work deals with very large

UNDERSTANDING BERNARD MALAMUD

themes painted on very small canvases. The ultimate case of this is *The Fixer* where the actions of an insignificant handyman in a wretched prison cell threaten the entire Russian Empire.

Malamud and his wife, the former Ann de Chiara, had spent a year in Italy in 1956, and this stay provided the background for half a dozen stories with Italian settings. In 1969, Malamud put three already collected stories about an art student named Arthur Fidelman together with three new ones to produce a series of vignettes called *Pictures of Fidelman*. The stories hold together well enough to form an episodic novel which traces Fidelman's career from art student to pretentious artist to serious artisan. The book is filled with comic misadventures that test Fidelman's commitment to both life and art. At the end of the novel, Fidelman no longer fiddles around with art but becomes faithful (shows his *fidelity*) to both love and his craft. The concern with art for its own sake and for its relation to life remains the concern of Malamud's next two works, *The Tenants* and *Rembrandt's Hat*.

The Tenants (1971) is Malamud's fiercest representation of his belief that men exist and define themselves only in terms of some other person. Here, as in some of the short stories, the bond is one of envy and hatred, though each emotion also contains the germ of grudging love. Theoretically, this is the ultimate Malamudian novel. Two men—one Jewish, one black, polar opposites—love each other, hate each other, support each other, and finally destroy each other. The novel is a theoretical success, but an emotional failure. The reader never

UNDERSTANDING BERNARD MALAMUD

cares about the characters, only about what they stand for. Interestingly in an interview given at the time this novel was published some of the book's ferocity of spirit seems to have seeped into its author. He talks about a page of fiction as if it were a living thing needing to be shaped into its ultimate form. "Either it bleeds and shows it's beginning to be human, or the form emits shadows of itself and I'm off. I have a terrifying will that way."[2]

Rembrandt's Hat (1973) is Malamud's third collection of short stories. Only one of the stories, "The Silver Crown," is in the mystical Yiddish mode of many of the stories in the earlier collections, and, in fact, one finds in this collection a new model, Chekhov (one of the characters in "Man in the Drawer" visits the Chekhov Museum). The title story in particular concerns itself with the same kind of social nuances that are found in Chekhov's stories like "Lady with Lapdog" and "Gooseberries." "Notes from a Lady at a Dinner Party," Malamud's story in which a successful architect trades childish mash notes with his former teacher's wife, exposes the same kind of boorishness that Chekhov derides in "The Kiss." Though the moral sphere is not neglected for the social in this collection, it is the first time that a reader is disappointed in one of Malamud's characters because he is a boor.

Malamud's two most recent novels, *Dubin's Lives* and *God's Grace*, show a magisterial command of the development of character and theme respectively. *Dubin's Lives* (1979) is almost eerily parallel to Philip Roth's *The Ghost Writer*, published in the same year. Both chronicle the late

UNDERSTANDING BERNARD MALAMUD

years of unhappily married writers who live reclusively in New England and have brief affairs with much younger women as they take stock of their careers and their lives. Actually the similarity is not so surprising, Malamud is a likely model for Roth's E. I. Lonoff, and Dubin, though a biographer rather than a novelist, is at least partially an autobiographical creation of Malamud's. Malamud denied that Dubin's life was his own, but admitted that he shared many of Dubin's concerns about life and art. Of the place of autobiography in his novels, he has said, "One must transcend autobiographical detail by inventing it after it is remembered."[3] In the novel, we see the mature genius of Malamud, creating a character who comes to terms both with his life (including love for his wife and his mistress) and with his lives—his career of writing the lives of others. Dubin learns to value his achievements, even as he learns to accept the limitations that both time and his own frailty impose upon him. Malamud saw the book as "his attempt at bigness, at summing up what he has learned over the long haul."[4]

In *God's Grace* (1982), Malamud tackles once more the big questions that have informed all his fiction. Malamud uses an allegory in which the last man on earth attempts to found a new society among a small group of apes who are the last hope for intelligent life on earth. In dealing with the nuclear holocaust and God's reasons for permitting it, even to the destruction of the last man, Malamud also faces up to the problem that has troubled his fiction for the last thirty years, the Nazi Holocaust and why it was permitted by God, and perhaps more importantly, by man. In an often comic vein, Malamud's hero, Calvin Cohn, wrestles seriously with the meaning of life, the purposes of God, and the ultimate fate of mankind. The absurdly wise answers would not be surprising to the author of *Notes from the Underground* and the Grand Inquisitor section of *The Brothers Karamazov*. Howard Harvitz in Malamud's story "The Man in a Drawer," is an intellectual tourist at the Dostoevsky and Chekhov museums in Moscow, but Malamud himself has clearly spent a longer time observing and learning from these masters.

Overview

Malamud's fiction is, first of all, moral. The actions of his characters matter to the world; so does their inaction. What makes this so significant for the reader is that Malamud's heroes begin as ordinary men—often even less than ordinary men. His characters cannot opt out by saying as Eliot's Prufrock did, "I am not Hamlet nor was meant to be." It is not necessary to be a prince to be significant. Dubin and Levin and Bok are men with no natural gifts, yet they acquire the courage to make difficult moral choices. This is not to say that Malamud's fiction fits a predetermined morality. Rather, most of his characters have to discover or build their own moral laws. At the heart of these moral laws is responsibility. Each man must determine his responsibility for himself and then for others.

UNDERSTANDING BERNARD MALAMUD

Malamud's characters are soldiers on a moral battlefield. Institutions, situations, other characters, even objects, become part of the moral landscape. In most cases, the moral issue is whether or not a character is what he appears to be, whether the character is willing to occupy the moral center of his universe or is content to skulk around its edges. Thus S. Levin, the hero of *A New Life*, is a humanities teacher who has to find out if he believes in humanity. He will fail or succeed as he takes on responsibility for other human beings. Albert Gans, in "The Silver Crown," teaches biology, the science of life; he will have to prove whether or not he believes in life. Though many of Malamud's heroes succeed at the moral level (almost all fail in material terms), some, like Gans, fail morally as well. Usually this failure occurs when the hero accepts a nominal triumph, that is, a way out by which he can say he has done the right thing even though he knows better. The temptation of a nominal triumph is everywhere in Malamud, and only a clear moral vision can keep the hero from mistaking bogus values from real ones.

Such moral battlegrounds are not the exclusive landscape of Malamud, but few writers, with the exception of Dostoevsky, have devoted themselves so exclusively to it. Also few writers have called so often on the weak to prove their courage. Malamud's heroes, like Yakov Bok, the title character of *The Fixer*, are the downtrodden of the world, and yet they must prove that they have greater moral strength than their oppressors. Unlike the heroes of Greek or Shakespearean plays, they begin at the bottom.

UNDERSTANDING BERNARD MALAMUD

Suffering, commitment, and responsibility are the hallmarks of Malamud's heroes. They are men who start with nothing before some system tries to make them into less than nothing. The greatest of these heroes grow stronger as their lives become more minimal. It is here suffering ennobles by building commitment to an ideal. Sometimes the ideal has independent validity, but more often the commitment itself gives an act its moral value. These acts of heroism, at their best, are not acts of self, but derive from or create responsibility toward another human being.

Always the characters find themselves morally linked to each other. Not only do the weak, like Frank Alpine in *The Assistant*, find themselves supporting the weaker (Bober), more surprisingly, the oppressors find themselves prisoners of their victims' determination. Grubeshov, the prosecutor in *The Fixer*, is in fact less free than his prisoner, and ends up begging Bok to compromise. Gilley, who holds the fate of Levin in his hands, is the one who ends up with no choices. And the tenants, in the novel of that name, finds that despite their mutual hatred, they can do nothing without each other.

Malamud's subject is nothing less that the meaning of life, and that meaning is built out of Martin Buber's concept of the I-thou relationship. Buber, the existential Jewish philosopher, argues that all significant relationships are built between the aware self, the "I," and one other person (loved and/or hated) intimate enough to be called "thou." If an individual can learn to establish such relationships, he may finally be able to relate to God, the ultimate Thou. Though the individual can engage in more than one such I-thou relationship, the relationship always retains its dual, rather than plural, character. In such a relationship, it is impossible to shift responsibility or blame. "I am responsible for thee" makes much tougher moral demands than "we are responsible for them." In the world of Malamud, a character must find out who he is and then discover for whom he is responsible.

As an artist himself Malamud often asks about the relationship of art to life. He asks again and again whether life imitates art or art imitates life. The answers are sometimes playful, as in *Pictures of Fidelman*, and sometimes serious, as in the stories in *Rembrandt's Hat*, but always the artist is nothing if he is not moral. The artist is a failure only if he excludes life from his art entirely. Fidelman has his entire life's work destroyed by the man whose wife he is sleeping with. Beppo's reason is not the adultery, but Fidelman's artistic failure for having spent his career slavishly imitating the work of others. Art also fails when it exhausts itself in pure theory. Fidelman has devoted himself to a suprematist mode of art in which the ultimate form is a square hole in the ground, emptiness organized, as it were. A mysterious stranger pushes Fidelman into his hole, giving substance to his form. Malamud himself has little patience with fiction that worries only about technique, and insists that the art of the novelist is "story, story, story."

When Malamud builds characters almost every detail is significant. Everything about them matters, beginning with their names. Often these names are allegorical, though they may have to be translated from another language to make

sense. Fidelman (Latin, *fidelis* 'faithful') in *Pictures of Fidelman*
is the man of faith (here as in Kierkegaard's *Fear and Trembling*, a faith to be tested). Roy Hobbs, in *The Natural*, is a
king and a bumpkin, as his first and last names imply. Yakov
Bok, whose last name means "goat," is the scapegoat in a plot
built up by Russian anti-Semites, and he is also the one kid in
the song at the end of the Passover Seder who survives ferocious predators throughout history. Often names contain literary allusions. S. Levin is the namesake of the hero of
Tolstoy's *Anna Karenina*, a man who strives for healthy, nor-
mal family life. Pop Fisher, the manager of the New York
Knights, in *The Natural*, is the Fisher King of the Grail legend.
Sometimes the wordplay in names is quite elaborate. Frank
Alpine is called the "assistant" rather than the more likely
"clerk" so that his name and job parallel exactly St. Francis of
Assisi. The fact that a character is named after a greater hero
does not mean that the character is the hero. Malamud's
names need to be tested against the action of the stories in
which they appear. Sometimes the comparisons are direct,
and sometimes they are ironical.

Physical characteristics have meaning. If a woman has a
sick or injured breast, it is suggested that she is incapable of
moral or psychological nurturing (Avis Fliss in *A New Life*
and Memo Paris in *The Natural*). If a man is physically infertile, he is often emotionally or spiritually infertile as well.
Similarly, characters with one eye or characters who look
through keyholes tend to be narrow-minded, and when a hero
injures an eye he loses his moral as well as his physical perspec-

tive. Such conditions are often found clustered in the novels, as when we hear about the eyes of Max Mercy, Judge Banner, Gus Sands, and Roy Hobbs in *The Natural*. Such physical attributes can be temporary or permanent, and the reader should watch for physical changes that stand for moral ones.

Malamud chooses the occupations of his characters with care. He never thinks of these occupations as jobs, but as professions or vocations in the root sense of these words. A profession is a statement of one's principles, and a vocation is a calling. Usually these occupations characterize their practitioners. Often a character is tested to see if he is worthy of the profession or business to which he belongs. There are many critics and teachers in this category. Malamud sees them as beginning without full commitment to their specialty. In the course of a story, they will have this commitment tested. Dubin, the biographer-hero of *Dubin's Lives*, will have his commitment to life, and especially to his own life, tested. The occupations of Malamud's heroes need not be professional to be professions. Bober, the grocer, is charged with feeding the hungry, even if he goes hungry himself doing it. Though he never quite recognizes it, grocering is something he has been called to do as surely as Christ has been called to feed multitudes with loaves and fishes. Bober is more sure of the "profession" of his occupation. He gives "credit" (Latin, *credere* 'to believe') to the poor as a statement of his belief in mankind.

The possessions of characters are also significant. If Roy Hobbs makes his bat out of a lightning-struck tree and keeps it in a bassoon case, all of these details have significance. If a character is casually seen reading a magazine, the title of the magazine should be noted as well as the picture on its front cover. In short, every detail, especially those that do not advance the plot, has significance, and the reader should watch these very carefully.

There are a number of recurring character types in Malamud. Almost always, Malamud's hero is the *Outsider*. The hero consistently enters an alien culture where both his own values and those of the society he enters are tested. Bok leaves his Jewish *shtetl* ('a country village') and takes up residence in the non-Jewish quarter of Kiev, Russia's Holy City. This leads to a test of both Bok's Jewishness and the Christianity of the inhabitants in Kiev. The hero can move the other way as well. Frank Alpine, in *The Assistant*, is a Catholic who lives among Jews, where he tests his Christianity, and surprisingly his Jewishness as well. Denizens of the city, like S. Levin, invade the country and vice versa (Roy Hobbs, the farm boy joins the New York Knights). Again, the values of both the man and the world he enters are tested.

Often opposed to the hero is the *Representative of an Institution*. Often these institutions stand in the abstract for virtues, but these virtues have become rigid and inhuman in practice. Fishbein in "Idiots First" refuses to do a small charitable act because he has institutionalized all his charity. Gilley, in *A New Life*, passionately believes he is serving his students' larger needs, by protecting them from the uncertainties of the humanities, and Bibikov, believes that the law he serves, and serves well, is more important than the men who are abused by it. The representatives of institutions believe that they are doing good in the world and often defend their actions and attitudes by impressive, though specious, arguments. It is up to the heroes to see through this kind of rationalization.

Women for the most part are minor characters in Malamud, important for the way they affect the hero rather than in their own right. They tend to be of two kinds. The *Nurturing Woman* provides support for the hero, usually when he has reached his lowest spiritual state. They tend to be Earth Motherly with an overlay of the spiritual. Usually by name, by metaphor, or by attributes, these women are associated with birds or flowers or fruit. Such figures are Iris Lemon in *The Natural* and Irene Bell in *The Tenants*. The hero may accept or reject the ministrations of these figures, though if he accepts, it is after an initial rejection.

The opposite number to this nurturing figure is the *Harpy*, the man-devouring woman, who offers the hero sex instead of love and is always involved in getting him to give up his principles. These women are almost always marked by some physical handicap—the sick breasts of Avis Fliss and Memo Paris or the limp of Zinaida in *The Fixer*. The hero frequently thinks that the offer of sex is a stroke of luck on his part, but unless he tears himself away from this woman and her temptations, he will be destroyed.

In his floundering toward moral truth, the hero takes on the characteristics of a figure from Jewish folktales, the *schlemiehl*, who can be seen most readily in the stories of I. B. Singer. The *schlemiehl* is a fool, a moral innocent in a world of shady operators. Always the operators take advantage of him—steal his money, sleep with his wife, trade him a broken down mule for his good cow—and yet at the end, we discover that the fool is stronger than the worldly wise men who deceive him. Malamud further defines folly by dividing his fools into *schlemiehls* and *schlimazels*. The *schlemiehl* is the passive victim, while the *schlimazel* tends to be an active agent. Trouble finds the *schlemiehl*, but the *schlimazel* looks for trouble. Often these characters run in pairs and contribute simultaneously to each other's bad luck and their moral virtue. Among the neatest of these *schlimazel/schlemiehl* pairs is Frank Alpine/Morris Bober and Roy Hobbs/Pop Fisher. Though both tend to attribute their material failure to bad luck, they usually suffer because of their honesty and trust in mankind. You don't have to be Jewish to be a *schlimazel*, and Parzival, the heroic knight who is too foolish to ask the right questions, fits the mold perfectly, as does Roy Hobbs, the character whose life is built on the Parzival archetype.

All these victims need victimizers, so Malamud peoples his novels with *worldly wise men* who take advantage of the fools. These characters, like Julius Karp in *The Assistant* or Gus Sands in *The Natural*, always seem to have good luck on their side, but usually they manufacture their luck by taking advantage of the weak and the poor. These men have a secret envy of the fools they bully or cheat and often feel the need, not merely to take advantage of their victims, but to impress them with their own "virtue" or skill. The symbiosis of opposites is one of the mainstays of human relationships in Malamud. The victimizers need their victims, not merely for profit, but also to affirm what they themselves are. The converse is also true: the victims need their victimizers, not out of masochism, but out of a need to fulfill their nature.

A character who seems at first closely related to the worldly wise man is the *imposter.* By pretending to be something he is not, the imposter leads the hero to the brink of some moral dilemma. Unlike the worldly wise men, these imposters are almost all poor men who live by their wits. They include Salzman, the marriage broker who has neither office nor magic barrel filled with dossiers of choice brides; Lifschitz, the maker of healing silver crowns; and almost all the guides in the Italian stories. The deceitfulness of these imposters is never the central moral issue of the stories in which they appear; instead, their imposture leads the hero to expose a more basic moral imposture. Sometimes the exposure is beneficial to the hero, more often it is harmful. Lifschitz, whose silver crowns may or may not be miracles, gets Gans to expose the real lie in the story, his pretense that he loves his father, and when the father of the Lady of the Lake shows Freeman fake works of art and pretends that his daughter is an Italian aristocrat, he exposes Freeman's moral duplicity. The imposters can bring out the best as well as the worst in men. Salzman's lie about his magic barrel gives Finkle the opportunity to develop the compassion he needs to be a rabbi. Though Finkle had protested when Salzman called him rabbi, he was little more than an imposter himself until the imposter made it necessary for him to find his vocation.

UNDERSTANDING BERNARD MALAMUD

In addition to human characters, Malamud's novels abound with supernatural ones, especially *angels* and *demons*. Some of these are traditional, but often they take on unconventional characteristics, like the title character of Angel Levine, a black man who is the guardian angel of a Jewish man. Quite often these supernatural beings look suspiciously human, until some slip gives them away. Ginzburg, the Angel of Death, in "Idiots First," is overwhelmed by the moral outrage of the hero, and Gus Sands, with his evil eye and his nightclub, the Pot of Fire, makes a perfectly plausible devil. Whatever their powers, however, these supernatural beings, like the devil who tormented Job, have no control over the inner or moral lives of the heroes, unless the heroes voluntarily give it up.

The presence of such characters, who often begin as distinctly human figures, is not surprising in Malamud's world, which is one of fable rather than realistic fiction. Though only two of the novels (*The Natural* and *God's Grace*, plus a number of the stories) have nonrealistic plots, almost all Malamud's fiction is fable. In such fiction all talk tends to become philosophical and all action symbolic. The characters tend to have elaborate symbolic dreams, metaphors become as real as the things they describe, and actions turn into rituals. Though such devices are to be expected in the myth of *The Natural*, they also dominate *The Assistant*, a novel whose surface is based largely on Malamud's memories of his father's grocery.

Malamud, unashamedly, has his characters discuss the meaning of life, of man's place in the universe, of his relation to God and men. Often this talk begins as homely, sentence-long aphorisms, particularly in the vein of Yiddish irony and world-weariness. Yakov Bok starts by lamenting cleverly about the way the world or God is treating him. By the end of *The Fixer*, his clever sayings have evolved into a philosophy complete enough to compare his view of religion, history, and politics with that of Spinoza. Morris Bober's willingness (in *The Assistant*) to trust a child for the price of a loaf of bread develops into a system of interpersonal faith as comprehensive as that of his near-namesake, Martin Buber. These philosophies are never divorced from the world and its inhabitants, but become the context in which moral, though often unprofitable, behavior exists.

Symbolism helps state indirectly what Malamud's characters say in their philosophies. The texture of fable provides a comfortable home for Malamud's symbolism. Characters dream almost as often as they wake, and their dreams provide meanings for symbolic objects clustered throughout each book. These symbols usually appear in patterns of meaning that follow such schemes as the change of the seasons, the conflict between country and city, between fertility and infertility, between masculine and feminine. Symbolic values are also built into the rich metaphoric language of Malamud's style, at times so dense that the literal meaning sinks below the figurative. Malamud often uses conventional archetypal patterns (the ritualistic behavior by which primitive societies mimic the original acts of the gods) found in Jung and Freud and Frazer. He gives mythic meaning to all sorts of primal acts

UNDERSTANDING BERNARD MALAMUD

so that eating often becomes feasting, and sometimes communion, sex becomes the union of two forces (sympathetic or antagonistic), and birth and death change from physical to spiritual events. All of which is to say that the acts of Malamud's characters, because they are moral agents, matter in way which far exceeds the literal significance of those acts.

Plot in Malamud is also moral. The protagonist will have a choice to make between two alternatives, each of which represents a set of moral values. Sometimes the hero is called on to make a yes/no choice and sometimes a this/that choice. These alternatives are not theoretical but experiential, so that the hero will have tried each of the alternatives before making his final decision. If there are two women to choose from, the hero will sleep with them both, eat their cooking, read their books. If the choice is between comfortable imprisonment or harsh freedom, the hero will try both. This makes experience knowledge in Malamud. Usually the alternatives are personal (dealing with love of some kind) or vocational (dealing with career or calling) or both.

Usually the choices open to the hero interact, considerably complicating the hero's decision and its meaning, so that, for example, S. Levin in *A New Life* must decide whether or not to love Pauline Gilley and whether or not to oppose the chairmanship of Gerald Gilley. Since the cuckolding of Gerald cannot be separated from Levin's opposition to his policies, Levin finds his choices have become Pauline/no-teaching or no-Pauline/teaching. This is the typical moral dilemma of Malamud's heroes. The only way to obtain one good is to sac-

UNDERSTANDING BERNARD MALAMUD

rifice another one. At his best, Malamud balances the scales so closely that only a fully developed moral character can choose wisely. Often when the wise choice is made, the character transforms a lesser virtue into a greater one or one virtue into its opposite. Bok becomes a better Jew by resisting the temptation to prevent a pogrom by his confession, and Frank Alpine becomes the perfect Christian when he gives up his Christianity and becomes a Jew. Malamud loves paradoxes of this kind, and often the conclusion of a novel depends upon the juggler's skill of keeping several sets of values in the air simultaneously, as when Dubin is loyal to Fanny by deserting her and most in love with his wife when he brings her the lust he has for his mistress, or when Calvin Cohn is sacrificed as Isaac and Jesus.

Because every extreme behavior creates the seeds of its polar opposite, paradox is not merely common, it is even necessary in Malamud. The moment of this discovery is one of fierce struggle, as when Mendel and the Angel of Death are throttling each other in "Idiots First". Each sees in the eyes of his opponent his own reflection, and ultimately the Angel of Death is defeated by the image of his own rage, even as Mendel sees the strength of his own charity.

One event, the Nazi Holocaust, eerily haunts much of Malamud's fiction, even though no stories or novels are set in the death camps. The smell of gas in Bober's apartment carries a hint of xyclon-B about it, and the threat of pogrom held over Bok's head foreshadows the greater anti-Semitism of half a century later. Hitler changes the way mankind thinks about itself. When the most civilized nation of its time set about to slaughter, torture, and mutilate Gypsies, Communists, Catholics, and six million Jews, and no one spoke out against it, the concept of human nature changed. If Swift's "Modest Proposal" to butcher Irish babies for meat and use their skin for gloves and boots had been proposed in Buchenwald in 1943, it would have been considered a viable scientific experiment rather than an allegorical fantasy. If the home of Beethoven, Bach, and the greatest assemblage of Nobel Prize winners could permit such inhumanity of man to man, then Cohn's attempts in *God's Grace* to civilize the savagery out of the apes by reading them Shakespeare (always a favorite in Germany) is hopeless.

In the back of his mind, Malamud has the familiar story of the man who stood by as the Nazis came for the Jews, then for the Catholics, then for the Communists, then for the intellectuals. When members of each group cried out for help, he remained silent. When they came for him, he cried out for help, but there was nobody left to hear. This is the basis for responsibility in Malamud, even for strangers. We are all responsible for one another, otherwise no one is responsible for us. Bessie, the baker's wife, who denies "The Loan" to her husband's friend so he can put a headstone on his wife's grave, should have known better. She is herself the sister of a victim of Hitler's ovens, and her husband has been sweetening his bread with the tears of affliction. Instead of granting the loan, however, she satisfies herself with the reasonable economics of relatively poor people—who knows what emergency might come up. As a sign of her failure to be charitable (to show her

UNDERSTANDING BERNARD MALAMUD

love for another human being, her married name is Lieb, German for love), the loaves in the oven are charred like Hitler's corpses. Just as the baker's tears bring sweetness to the loaf, so there is a strength to be gained by ultimate suffering, a strength seen in the shoemaker's apprentice, Sobel, for whom "The First Seven Years" of silent waiting for Feld's daughter are nothing after his years in the concentration camps.

Though some kinds of strength can be drawn from the Holocaust, Malamud is never far from the question it raises. Why did men let it happen? Why did God let it happen? Why did it happen to the Jews? Were the Chosen People chosen only for their suffering? What can the individual man do in the face of such suffering? How does one deal with the fact that it has happened? As Malamud deals with the answers to such questions he expands his moral concerns from those of Jews to those of all mankind. The reader must always know that being human carries two moral imperatives, one of strength and one of weakness, "I suffer for you" and "I am responsible for you." The final step recognizes that these two statements are one and that the Jew who embodied this duality was the Savior of the Christians.

UNDERSTANDING BERNARD MALAMUD

Notes

1. Israel Shenker, "Bernard Malamud on Writing Fiction," *Writer's Digest*, July 1972: 22.

2. Shenker: 23.

3. Ralph Tyler, "A Talk with the Novelist," *New York Times Book Review* 18, February 1979: 1.

4. *Ibid.*

CHAPTER TWO

THE NATURAL

Malamud's first novel, *The Natural* (1952), is a fable in which the fortunes of its hero, a baseball player named Roy Hobbs, parallel those of Parzival, the medieval knight who restored the Wasteland. Since this is a fable, the characters tend to be two-dimensional, existing more for their meaning than for themselves. Almost all have names that indicate their function, and Malamud is not particularly subtle about superimposing the medieval story upon the modern setting. The novel is enriched by drawing on events out of baseball lore and legend, like the 1949 hotel room shooting of Philadelphia Phillies infielder Eddie Waitkus by a crazed female sports fan (Waitkus came back the following year to lead the Phillies to their first pennant in forty years), the infamous Black Sox Scandal of 1919, the many achievements of Babe Ruth, and the fate of "Casey at the Bat."

Roy Hobbs, the aging rookie who comes up to play for the hapless New York Knights is both a fool and a hero. The medieval Parzival was also a country bumpkin who made a fool of himself trying to make sense of the sophisticated ways of knighthood. His move from the country to the court parallels Roy's move from the country to New York City. Almost all of Malamud's heroes follow this pattern of moving from the most congenial to the most alien environment available.

The novel's title repeats the duality implicit in Roy's role. A "natural" in baseball jargon is a player with outstanding natural talent, but to the Middle Ages, a "natural" was an innocent fool. The notion behind this meaning of "natural" was that after Adam's fall, man fell away from his proper nature and declined into mere worldly wisdom. The natural, touched by God, retained his Edenic nature and seemed a fool to the rest of mankind. Though armed with a natural goodness, the natural was easy prey to the worldly wise if he strayed from his God-given intuitions.

After he became a knight, Parzival was given the quest of finding and healing the Fisher King of the Wasteland, whose land had remained barren ever since he received a wound from the same spear that wounded Christ's side. In order to succeed, Parzival must ask a question of the Fisher King, but the knight's too-rigid interpretation of newly learned chivalric courtesy keeps him silent. According to the chivalric code, Parzival has failed his quest forever. Instead of accepting this conclusion, Parzival breaks the letter of the law to find its spirit. Though he is told he has already lost, Parzival tries again, and through persistence alone succeeds in a second, long-delayed attempt to heal the Fisher King.

In an episode parallel to Parzival's first unsuccessful quest, Roy at nineteen comes up for a try in the big leagues as

THE NATURAL

a pitcher. He is good enough to strike out (in an exhibition) the reigning slugger, Whammer Wambold, on three pitches, but his bid ends when he is shot in the gut by a mystery woman named Harriet Bird. Though the sensual description of the scene in which he is shot by the naked woman suggests that the reason for his failure is his yielding to sexual temptation, the primary reason seems to be his inability to answer Harriet's question about what he hopes to accomplish in his career. When he can think of nothing more than the satisfaction of personal glory, Harriet plans to shoot him as she has shot other athletes who were the best in their sports. It is not enough for the hero to have talent, he must have a purpose in his life. This changes the preliminary episode in Parzival where the hero fails because he does not ask, rather than answer, the right question. Nonetheless, the basis for failure is much the same: both heroes are too wrapped up in their self-image to recognize the awesome responsibility that comes with their great talent.

Though she has little more than a bit part, Harriet Bird's presence broods over the entire novel. As one who will destroy a hero rather than have him waste his gifts, she is the spiritual ancestor of the two women who will be rivals for Roy's love. For this reason, Malamud puts the symbols for both women—white roses for Iris, the hero-nurturer, and a black-feathered hat for Memo, the hero-destroyer—in Harriet's hotel room. Furthermore, birds as signs of Roy's fate (bird flight was used by the Greeks and Romans to predict the future) are everywhere in the novel. When Whammer faces

UNDERSTANDING BERNARD MALAMUD

Roy's best pitch, it looks like a bird in flight, when Roy becomes too intent on proving his ability he catches (and kills) a canary instead of the ball, the hamburgers that spell Roy's doom at an ill-fated feast look like dead birds, and the opposing pitchers in the final game, Vogelman and Fowler (who is a traitor to the Knights) are both named for birdcatchers. Birds will remain a favorite symbol of Malamud's, though they will prove almost always positive after this novel.

After fifteen years, Roy returns to baseball, this time as a home-run hitter rather than a pitcher (Babe Ruth, the game's greatest slugger, began as a pitcher and held the record for consecutive scoreless innings in the World Series). This time he joins the New York Knights, a team so bad even its ballfield, like the Wasteland, suffers from drought. Its manager Pop Fisher is the Fisher King whose wound is the impossible affliction, athlete's foot of the hands. According to one theory the Fisher King's name comes from a misinterpretation of the French original in which the king was *Le Roi Pécheur*, the Sinner King, rather than *Le Roi Pêcheur*, the Fisher King. As the Sinner King, the ruler of the Wasteland is the man who represents all the sins of his people, and his land cannot become fertile until he is replaced by a young, innocent hero (a similar myth in modern dress is found in Saul Bellow's novel, *Henderson, the Rain King*). Normally the Sinner King has committed some sin that is representative of his people's sinfulness. In Pop's case, it is Fisher's Flop, a bonehead play from his own playing days that cost his team the pennant. Since then his luck has left him, and he has spent a career without winning a

THE NATURAL

pennant. Roy is the man who can undo this bad luck and bring relief to the drought. When he starts hitting, torrential rains come down and the field turns green.

As bringer of fertility, Roy is also a phallic hero whose homemade bat, Wonderboy, becomes the symbol of his manhood. When Roy goes into a slump, the bat actually droops. As fertility god, Roy has to choose the proper woman to be his consort, and, as in much of Malamud, the hero has a choice between a woman who represents life-giving fertility and one whose power lies in her seductive vanity. Iris Lemon, named for a fruit and a flower (two powerful positive symbols in Malamud's work), is the woman whom Roy should choose. The other woman is Memo Paris, whose last name suggests Helen who was abducted to Troy by Paris (Helen is also the name of the heroine in Malamud's next novel, *The Assistant*). That the women are polar opposites is designated first by their appearance. Memo is a red-haired woman who wears black, and Iris is a black-haired woman first seen wearing a red dress and a white rose.

Though Roy is attracted to Memo because of her beauty, her main appeal seems to be that she is the girl of Bump Bailey, the outfielder he must replace if he is to make a name for himself in baseball. Through a series of mix-ups, Roy sleeps with Memo almost as soon as he meets her, but thereafter she puts him off. Roy believes that Memo has mistaken him for Bump and never suspects that Bump, fearing Roy's abilities, has sent Memo to sap his strength and ruin his concentration. Despite his considerable abilities, Roy does not get Bump's place in the lineup until Bump kills himself chasing a fly ball into the out-field wall. Though Roy is literally innocent of Bump's death, he had taunted the usually lazy outfielder into playing harder, and so he has at least some responsibility in getting rid of his rival.

As it turns out, Bump's death does not clear the way for Roy in Memo's affections. Memo does not need Bump's urging to bring out the worst in Roy. She is a seductress who uses her powers to unman the men in her life. She seems to love Bump more after his death than she did when he was alive, and her statement to Roy that she is a "dead man's girl" describes a per-sonality rather than a fact. Her first name suggests she is someone who uses memory to live in the past.

Memo's dwelling on past glory carries the odor of the grave with it. Her condition is symbolized by her sick breast, a sign that she is incapable of either nurturing the hero or bearing her own offspring. She is inimical to life in every way. After Roy discovers the sick breast in a frustrating tryst, Memo drives off doing ninety miles an hour with the lights off. When Roy finally convinces her to turn the lights on, they think they see a boy on the side of the road, and there is a thud as if they have hit someone. Memo refuses to stop, and Roy believes they have killed a child, even though there is no blood on the car. Roy suffers terrible guilt over this crime that may have no substance at all.

Memo is a creator of illusions, while Iris is all substance. Iris is connected with Roy's first selfless act, which also con-cerns a boy injured in an auto accident. Roy promises the in-

THE NATURAL

jured boy, who has given up struggling for his life, that he will hit a home run for him (the incident is taken from the career of Babe Ruth). Roy understands for the first time that as a baseball hero he is not an independent agent, but has become responsible for another human being. The hitting of the home run occurs at the nadir of his season when he is not hitting because he is frustrated about his affair with Memo and feels guilty about the boy he may have hit on the road. Roy's slump reflects his wilted self-image, but, when Iris stands up in the stands for him, he responds by hitting the ball so hard that it goes into the stands after going under the second baseman's legs.

Iris's interest is more than personal. She makes positive sense of Harriet Bird's destructive interest in heroes. She urges upon Roy the responsibility, evidenced in hitting the home run for the boy, inherent in being a hero. A hero does not merely defend the weak and lift the downtrodden, he becomes a moral exemplar for ordinary people, and especially for children. The response when Shoeless Joe Jackson took bribes to throw the 1919 World Series was one of a people who had lost its hero, "Say it ain't so, Joe." A whole generation of boys had lost a role model.

Iris tries to explain to Roy the sacrifice of ego that is required of a hero. The hero is not for himself, but for others. Without selflessness, the hero becomes nothing more than a star like Bump Bailey. Iris explains her own sacrifice when she stood up in front of thousands of fans for Roy. She had given up her shy persona so that Roy would have an object upon which to project his ego, and it had worked. By relating his self to another person he was able to free himself from the prison of self, and by drawing strength from his concern for Iris he was able to draw strength from the whole crowd she represented. This is an example of the I-thou relationship described by the Jewish existential philosopher, Martin Buber. In this relationship the self paradoxically becomes most itself when it turns away from its own concerns and develops an honest relationship with another. This relationship must be open enough so that the other is considered the personal "thou" rather than the social "you." When the self can do this the masks of ego are no longer needed, and the I realizes itself.

Iris becomes Malamud's spokesman as she explains to Roy the theory that every person has two lives: one life teaches through experience how to live, and the other life is the life lived out of that knowledge. The life that teaches is always built out of suffering and sacrifice so that the life that is lived can move toward happiness by choosing the right things. What Iris doesn't tell the impatient Roy is that we always live on the edge between these two lives, that the road to happiness is never more than one moment beyond the life of suffering. Among Malamud's heroes, only two men, William Dubin the biographer, and Yakov Bok the fixer, fully understand this truth.

Iris can bring Roy to the life that teaches only by freeing him from his fear of mortality. She must make him see that playing baseball with the aim of making himself immortal by

THE NATURAL

setting records is both immoral and self-centered. She can do this only if she can counter Roy's fear that he will grow old before he can make his mark. Roy knows that Pop Fisher's career lasted till he was only a year older than Roy is now. Though Roy sees Pop partly as a father figure, he also sees in Pop an image of himself. Roy fears the transition from being the wielder of Wonderboy to becoming himself Pop Hobbs. Though he sees Iris as more fruitful than Memo, he retreats from her proffered love when she tells him that at thirty-three she is a grandmother. He can only conclude that if he marries her, it would make him a grandfather.

The lakeside consummation of Roy's affair with Iris contains all possibilities: lust, love, death, rebirth, and birth. Roy, who can never forget Harriet Bird (and there have been other "Harriets" in his fifteen-year exile), denies the intuition of his heart and treats the selfless Iris with the callous lust more appropriate to Harriet or Memo. Iris is repulsed by his boorish "Give us a kiss," and when she turns him away, he dives to the bottom of the lake where he would be content to stay embraced by the death he has feared so long. Iris sees his dive to the bottom as either the same impulse that makes him want to set batting records or as a simple act of sexual frustration. She does not realize it is a suicidal act of black despair. Her love conquers her revulsion for his selfish behavior, and she brings him up from the depths. She no longer holds anything back, and he realizes that he has never known such a generous, giving woman, but as they make love she lets slip the fatal fact that she is a grandmother. Roy ignores the greater truth that he is the first man she has ever loved and that she is more virgin than grandmother.

Even as she is not able to plumb the depths of Roy's despair, Iris also makes the mistake of Parzival by failing to ask the right question. In the next to last sentence in the chapter, she begins to ask "are you . . . ?" but never finishes. Though there are many ways to end the sentence, at least one has to do with taking birth control precautions, a remark which might have alerted Roy to the possibility that a child is being conceived on this night.

After giving up Iris, Roy turns to other means of guaranteeing his immortality. When Roy feels the demons of old age weakening his arms and legs, he smashes a hit into the clock on the outfield wall, scattering time everywhere. It is a futile symbolic gesture, and soon Roy is dreaming of another kind of immortality, a son—a red-headed son of his and Memo's. This dream is just as futile as smashing the clock. He has chosen the infertile woman to be the mother of his children.

While Roy is getting his priorities confused with women, he has become enmeshed in the world of evil that surrounds the Knights baseball team. The evil characters all have trouble with their eyes, signifying that they are all suffering from some kind of moral blindness. The ill-named Max Mercy (we see him refusing to give charity to a beggar) is a sports writer whose column, "Through the Keyhole," tells of his one-eyed obsession with finding the worst in anyone. Mercy only sees the bad side of anyone's personality and is not content until he

THE NATURAL

can find Roy's dirty little secret. It is not until last page of the novel that Mercy uncovers the Harriet Bird affair and prints the story of a young man shot by a naked woman as if it were all that need be said of Roy. He ignores the sense of tragic waste in Roy's career, which is summed up by a woman who says he "coulda been a king."

Judge Goodwill Banner, part owner of the baseball team, suffers from a kind of myopia that is a generalized version of Mercy's. Instead of looking for the individual sin in each person, Banner assumes the corruption of the human race and has lived in spiritual darkness so long that light hurts his eyes. His only goal in life is to make a few cents out of the baseball team, and he will even sacrifice the pennant if it will garner him a profit. Banner is so cheap that he uses a maternity hospital to care for his players, and when Roy is sent there, the pain in his belly becomes a grotesque travesty of labor pains.

Gus Sands (his name reinforces his Satanic character; he is the August Prince of the desert place) owns a night club called the Pot of Fire whose chorus girls are devils with pitch forks. Gus is a one-eyed gambler with a glass eye that he says controls all luck. In his confrontation with Roy, he is the Supreme Bookie against the Super Rookie. Though he says the eye brings him luck, it is an evil eye that is meant to bring bad luck to his enemies. Furthermore, Sands does not really believe in luck at all, but rather manipulates events so they will turn out as he calls them. This is the reason Sands pays off Roy to blow the pennant game.

Roy succumbs to Sands's evil eye, though the reader is reminded that Roy could be more powerful than the bookie if he chose to believe in his own powers. After he loses six hundred dollars to Gus in a series of bets, Roy uses lightning quick sleight of hand to make six hundred silver dollars appear out of a table cloth. His hand is quicker than Sands's eye. Roy is capable of making his own luck, but doesn't believe it until too late. After he has sold out to the gambler and thrown the pennant game, Roy knocks out Gus's glass eye, which rolls away into a mousehole.

Roy's after-the-fact victory tells what he could have been if he had not succumbed to the superstitions so rife among baseball players, to the blandishments of Memo Paris, and especially to the fear of his own mortality. As lust for Memo begins to erode his skills, Roy becomes like the men he should oppose. He is afraid he is losing his eyesight and stops reading and starts sitting in the dark. He uses a number of good luck charms, but when he is no longer convinced of their efficacy, he decides to bet on the sure thing and take the bribe to throw the last game of the season.

Though Roy has had a great season, the judge refuses to give him any more money than is specified in his contract. Memo, apparently working for Sands, says she will marry Roy, but only if he has enough money. She uses her own fear of mortality to justify this need for money; she doesn't want to be poor so that she will be afraid of what the future might bring. She urges him to get enough money to buy a restaurant (the traditional occupation for retired baseball players) so

THE NATURAL

that they will have enough money for the future and also so they can feed the multitudes. Her fears correspond to Roy's, and he goes along when he feels like an old man without a future in baseball.

In the medieval poem, *Piers Plowman*, the poet says "All is not good for the ghost that the gut asketh," a phrase that perfectly describes the way Roy's appetites destroy his spirit. After his lust for Harriet Bird brings him to her hotel room, Roy is shot in the gut. When his lust for Memo overcomes his love for Iris, he is taken by Memo to a feast where he almost eats himself to death on bad (perhaps poisoned) food. His failure at the feast, like Parzival's, reduces him from the hero with supernatural gifts to that of an ordinary man with ordinary skills. Even so, the evil characters fear him and buy him out with the money that supposedly will make Memo his.

As Roy follows the plan to blow the pennant, he tries to sublimate his rage by hitting his greatest heckler, a dwarf named Otto Zipp, with a batted ball. Roy is such a good hitter that he is able to hit Zipp in the head with a foul ball even against the opponent's best pitcher, Vogelman. The ball, however, ricochets off Zipp's head and hits Iris, who, despite his coldness, has returned to root for him. Roy realizes he is in love with her even before she tells him that she is pregnant with the heir he has wanted to carry on his name. Roy goes out to win one for his son, for Pop, for the team, for Iris, but he is on his own. Wonderboy, his magical bat, breaks, and the hero is left to defend himself with an ordinary Louisville Slugger (even Arthur could be defeated when he lost Excalibur).

Nonetheless, he is ready to take on Vogelman, and, in fact, is so fearsome at the plate, has such a look of power in his eyes, that Vogelman faints dead away. Instead of the veteran, Roy faces a rookie named Youngberry, and the cycle takes another turn. Just as the powerful Roy struck out Whammer on three straight pitches, so the new young hero strikes out slugger Hobbs. There is no joy in Mudville, Mighty Casey has struck out.

CHAPTER THREE

THE ASSISTANT

I n *The Natural*, the characters are mythic at both levels: the literal story of the baseball season and the archetypal level of the Grail myth. Even though sometimes based on real people and no matter how fascinating or how sharply drawn, these are characters who never were. They are literary characters who have never dwelt beyond the covers of a book. This is not true of Malamud's second novel, *The Assistant* (1957), in which the novelist settles brilliantly into the mode that will inform most of his best fiction. The world of the grocery store is real, and its characters are flesh and blood. Malamud knows this world well. His father ran a grocery store not unlike Bober's, and Malamud's first published story in high school was an account of his own life "behind the counter."

The characters live and breathe the small lives of the most ordinary men, but what is extraordinary is that Malamud has also invested them with the mythic stature he had given his baseball players. This is partially because these characters have very carefully worked out mythic antecedents, but more because Malamud has made their every act meaningful. They are capable of deeds of courage and cowardice, hard-heartedness and compassion, worthy of the greatest of heroes.

In *The Assistant*, Malamud again retells medieval myth in a modern setting. This time, however, he counterpoints the Wasteland myth found in *The Natural* against the history of St. Francis of Assisi. Both medieval archetypes center around a pair of characters: Parzival and the Fisher King, Amfortas, in the first, and Francis and Christ in the second. The novel's principal characters, Frank Alpine and Morris Bober, find themselves in a set of antithetical relationships. Frank Alpine, a man who comes from San Francisco, whose favorite book is *The Little Flowers* (a medieval collection of vignettes of St. Francis), who is first seen feeding birds in the park (the saint loved birds so much he preached to them), will become St. Francis to Morris Bober's Christ. In this relationship, the morally weak Frank will learn from Bober's spiritual strength. In the Wasteland myth, however, Bober, is Amfortas, the maimed Fisher King who is waiting to be restored by Frank's Parzival. On this level, the despondent Bober will be cured by the energetic Frank.

St. Francis, the son of a wealthy cloth merchant, turned his back on his father's material possessions to enter the monastic life where he embraced poverty so completely that his followers were called Pauvres Frères ("impoverished brothers"). In giving up worldly wealth, he turned his back on the flesh and its pleasures, particularly, food and women. He was

THE ASSISTANT

known for his fasts and would go off for weeks with a minimal amount of bread and water and return with half his supplies intact. In giving up the wealth of world, he was following literally Christ's admonition to "sell all you have and follow me." In all he did, Francis's aim was the imitation of Christ. His ultimate reward was the appearance of the stigmata, the five wounds of Christ, on his body. The stigmata signified that he had learned to suffer like Christ for mankind. In the novel, Morris is wounded in the robbery staged by Frank and the detective's son, Ward Minogue. This wound doubles as the Fisher King's wound and the original stigmata of Christ. Frank first appears to have stigmata when he scratches his hands with his nails in his frustrated desire for Helen, but the ultimate stigmata occur at the end of the novel when he is circumcised, making him a Jew like Bober.

When Frank first appears in Bober's grocery, he is filled with the same worldly appetites that Francis had to give up. Frank steals food, and even looks upon Bober's daughter Helen with "hungry eyes." Little by little, Frank learns to govern and then give up his appetites. This restraint is not a negative or limiting attitude, but is converted into a positive activity, feeding the poor, which he learns from the example of Bober. At the very beginning of the novel, Bober, standing under his No Trust (no credit) sign gives food on credit to a drunken woman he knows will never repay him. Later, Frank performs the same duty when he goes to collect a bad debt from Carl, the Swedish painter. Seeing the man's poverty, he forgives the debt just as Bober would do, though he still has much to learn about the extent of Bober's powers of forgiveness. Eventually, Frank feeds the hungry day and night by turning the grocery into an all-night restaurant and working in a diner by day to help pay Bober's bills. By this time, he, like the saint, has almost stopped eating entirely.

Frank also learns to restrain his sexual appetites. When St. Francis was wondering about his decision to become a friar, he built himself a snow woman and snow children and declared that they were all the family he needed because he was going to put the flesh behind him. Frank tells Helen this story, but she takes it in a self-centered way and begins to think of herself as an idealized snow woman whose chastity is her only valuable possession. After Frank forces himself upon Helen the night he rescues her from attempted rape, Helen wraps herself in the snow woman's mantle and looks on Frank with an icy face while Frank dreams of looking at her through a frozen window. From this stage of self-revulsion on his side and rejection on hers, Frank's love for Helen changes from appetitive lust to a love that is more responsibility than anything else.

As the maimed Fisher King in the Parzival legend, Morris Bober laments the fact that he cannot even feed his family, just as the king of the Wasteland cannot feed his people. Like Pop Fisher in *The Natural*, Morris attributes his failure to bad luck. Though his luck is bad, the real reason he fails is that he is too honest to take advantage of anyone. He continues to give credit to the poor and refuses to cheat his customers.

THE ASSISTANT

In his honesty and bad luck, Morris is contrasted with a neighboring shopkeeper, Julius Karp, a liquor store owner, who seems always to have good luck. Morris never realizes that most of Karp's luck is manufactured by his selfishness. In the robbery that opens the novel's action, Karp, who is afraid his liquor store is about to be robbed, goes to Bober to let him know he might want to use his telephone (Karp, the richer man, is too cheap to have a telephone) to call the police. The obligation to remain open in case Karp returns freezes Bober in the store, while Karp runs off and leaves Bober as the robbers' only victim.

Karp also keeps renting an empty storefront to rival grocers on Bober's block, even though he knows the neighborhood cannot support two groceries. Though Karp pleads financial hardship, he makes it clear he would leave the store empty if his son Louis married Helen. Only self-interest can make Karp charitable. The wonder of their relationship is that Karp appreciates Bober's virtue more than Bober does himself, and often finds ways to spend time with Bober, if only to be in the presence of such goodness. This contact with goodness does not, however, change Karp at all.

Bober, on the other hand, never takes advantage of anyone. When a poor immigrant is about to buy his wretched store, Bober cannot keep his mouth shut, and by telling him the truth about the store's meager earnings frightens off the potential buyer. Not only does Morris refuse to cheat the poor, he doesn't even feel jealous of the success of his ex-partner, Charlie Sobeloff, who has bilked him out of four thousand dollars and used the money to start a successful supermarket.

Morris's despair comes from the fact that he does not appreciate the value of his own virtue and charity. Though he despises the values of Karp, the worldly wise man, who makes his living selling brain-destroying alcohol rather than life-giving milk, Bober still measures his own success by Karp's standards, and seen on those terms, the little grocery is a wasteland as barren as Amfortas's.

The Wasteland can only be restored if a pure, but foolish, knight comes to the Grail feast where he must ask the right question. The question is different in different versions of the myth, but usually has to do with the nature of the king's wound or the meaning of the feast. In the legend, Parzival finds Amfortas, is too overwhelmed by decorum to ask the question, and is sent away after being told he has failed his quest forever. Parzival, too "foolish" to accept this judgment, finds the Fisher King again, asks the question, heals the Fisher King, takes his place, and the land is restored.

Frank makes much the same mistakes as Parzival. His mindless eating in the store is the same as Parzival's presence at the initial Grail feast. Frank does ask the questions, "What is a Jew?" and "Why do you suffer?" but he is not wise enough to understand the apparently simple answers, "a Jew is a good man" and "I suffer for you." Like Parzival, his intentions are good, but he is not ready to assume the place of the king and is thrown out when he makes a foolish mistake. Frank begins his virtuous life by putting back some of the money he has stolen from Morris. Morris catches Frank stealing Frank's own money, but doesn't realize it. He fires his assistant just at the moment that Frank has begun his reformation. This is the fate of men like Frank: every time he tries to do a good deed, it turns out wrong. He has yet to learn that the nature of the deed is more important than its result.

Frank's virtue, instead of easing Morris's despair, therefore, increases it, because Morris feels he has lost the "son" he thought he had found in Frank. At the same time, new rival grocers have driven Morris's business down to nothing, and he turns on the gas and "accidentally" forgets to light it. Frank rescues Morris and resumes his job while Morris recuperates. The gas-filled store becomes Morris's self-created gas chamber as he dreams the rival Norwegian grocers are speaking German. Between the apparent betrayal of Frank, his daughter's indiscretions with the assistant, and Karp's renting to the Norwegians, Morris becomes convinced of man's infinite inhumanity to man. Since he might as well have become a victim of the Nazis, he allows the gas to destroy his spirit, his breath of life.

Though Frank has saved his life, Bober has hardened his heart against him and refuses to let him stay, even after Frank confesses his part in the holdup. Bober already knew this, and it is not the original crime that makes him refuse the assistant. Bober wants Frank to stay, but is not yet Christlike enough to turn the other cheek. He had accepted the robbery that occurred when Frank was a stranger and desperate. He cannot accept the subsequent petty theft in the store (even though it is finished) because this time Frank had asked to be trusted. For Morris, the breakdown of trust is the breakdown of one man's responsibility for another.

When Frank finds out that Bober had known for a long time that he was one of the robbers, he begins to understand what Bober means by saying, "I suffer for you." In fact, Frank understands Bober better than Bober understands himself. By knowing about Frank's crimes without revealing them or using them for moral leverage, Bober has taken responsibility for Frank's life and suffers for him the way Christ suffered for mankind. Since Christ was crucified for our sins, the pain of his crucifixion is increased every time man sins. When Frank realizes this, he knows that he must take up Morris's burden in the store as Morris had taken up his burden of sin. In doing this, he learns what St. Francis had learned about taking up the burdens of Christ.

The two heroes continually counterpoint each other's successes and failures. Just when Frank understands the nature of his own temptations, Bober falls victim to temptation of another kind. Malamud injects one of his eerie otherworldly figures, a Satanic firesetter who offers Bober a way out of the store: a fire that will let him collect his insurance. The fire-starter seems more a primeval representation of Bober's despair than another person. For this reason it hardly matters that Bober's strong moral sense allows him to repel the man's temptation. He finally yields to his own despair and tries to start the fire himself using a photographic negative as a fuse.

THE ASSISTANT

The burning negative symbolizes the absolute collapse of Bober's self-image. Once again Frank saves him, as he did from the gas and, at the beginning of the novel, when he collapsed carrying boxes in the snow. Though Morris still will not let him work in the store, Frank realizes that he is responsible for Morris and his family and knows that his only future is in the grocery. Morris's message, "I suffer for you," is beginning to be Frank's watchword as well.

Malamud marks the changes in his characters lives with elementary forces that take on the value of primitive ritual. Morris has to contend with ice and fire and then with fire and ice. A second fire after the one he tried to start seems to promise new hope. After watching his life go from one desperate moment to another, Morris suddenly thinks that his luck is beginning to change. A fire caused in a robbery attempt at Karp's liquor store burns down the Karp establishment, and the well-insured Karp begins negotiations to buy Bober's store so he can reopen his liquor business. For the first time, Bober sees hope for his family and in his high spirits goes out to shovel a late spring snow. The day, appropriately, is the day before April Fool's Day, and it is Bober who is the fool. The deceptive spring day is still wintry enough to give Bober a fatal case of pneumonia. Bober dies believing that his family will be provided for, but even this is a false hope. Karp suffers a heart attack, and since his lazy son doesn't want to keep up with the business, he never does buy Morris's store.

It would seem that Morris's life is a failure, but his funeral proves just the opposite. A favorite notion of Malamud's is one he borrows from Montaigne, "We should not judge of a man's happiness until after his death." To his wife and daughter, Morris's funeral seems to be a sham. His eulogy is delivered in extravagant terms by a rabbi who has never met him, but as Frank listens, he discovers that the rabbi is right: Bober's life has made a difference to all it touched.

Helen throws a rose into Morris's grave, and when Frank leans over to see what it is, he falls into the grave. Frank's rising from Morris's grave completes his symbolic rebirth and makes him into the new ruler of the Wasteland. His complete devotion to the store and his hard work make it, if not a wonderful success, at least a going concern.

Frank's "inheritance" of the grocery store turns him into the son Bober had long missed. Bober's own son, Ephraim had died of an unexplained ear infection, and with his death all of Bober's hopes beyond survival had also died. The Morris/ Frank–father/son relationship is paralleled by three other pairs of fathers and sons. Each of the sons is "romantically" linked to Helen, and each corresponds to one of the four kinds of sons named in the Passover Seder, which is like the Grail story, a feast whose center is the asking of questions. The four sons are the wise son, the wicked son, the foolish son, and the son who wits not to ask. The wise son is Nat Pearl, who was Helen's lover at one time. Nat is the son who fulfills the immigrants' dream of surpassing his parents in wealth and wisdom and becoming fully assimilated in the new land. Nat is on his way to becoming a successful lawyer, though he manages to ignore the Law of his people to do it. The foolish son is Louis

THE ASSISTANT

Karp, who is romancing Helen at the beginning of the story. He is the son who is too lazy to go into his father's successful business and will clearly do less well than his father without any compensating gain in morality. The wicked son is Ward Minogue, the son of a policeman. Minogue is Frank's partner in the robbery and the man who attempts to rape Helen in the park. Minogue tries to get Frank to return to his life of crime, and he represents what Frank might have become without the influence of Bober. Minogue is so outraged by Frank's decision to work in the grocery that he calls him a "kike" long before Frank even thinks about becoming a Jew. Ward is the son who disappoints his father in every way, so that when Morris discovers that it is Minogue who hit him on the head, his concern is not with revenge of any kind but rather with pity for the father. Frank, like Parzival, is the son who wits not to ask, though he finally overcomes this limitation and does ask the right questions. Frank eventually surpasses each of these sons and becomes more of a blessing to his "father" than they are. Unlike Louis Karp, he does take over his father's business, thereby leaving Bober's mark on society. He also learns the law as Pearl does, but it is the Jewish Law which Nat has forgotten. Frank even mimics Ward's defiance of his father, but only in refusing to listen when Morris warns him not to take over the store.

Frank's education in the grocery business is paralleled by the changes in his love for Bober's daughter, Helen. The romance of Frank and Helen finds two unsatisfied idealists yearning unhappily for each other. The two of them are idealistic both in what they want for themselves and in what they want in a beloved. Helen, stuck in her job at the Levenspiel bra factory, wants to be a college-educated person and is looking for a man with the same credentials. When she begins imagining herself in love with Frank, she dreams of a better-dressed, college-educated Frank with a smaller nose. To the end of the novel, she will not commit herself completely to Frank because she will not let go her dream of the ideal man, even the ideal Frank, coming along.

Frank also fosters a false self-image. Convinced he is a failure in life, he sees himself compensating by pursuing a glamorous life of crime, the kind of life projected in Hollywood gangster epics. This dream is dashed when his reward for his first "job" is half the take from Bober's grocery, half of fifteen dollars. Frank does have another ideal in mind, however, the St. Francis who had comforted him ever since his days in the orphanage. It is not until he establishes a proper relationship with both Helen and her father that he considers Francis a hero to be emulated.

Since both lovers are idealists who use the library as a trysting place, it is not surprising that their reading habits help define their idealism. Helen reads fiction, particularly epic tragedies of suffering like *Anna Karenina* and *Madame Bovary*. Helen would like to share the martyrdom of these heroines, but she fears the absolute commitment that destroys Anna and Emma. She tends toward self-dramatization, and her joyless life in the bra factory is boring, but hardly tragic. She crosses off the days on the calendar, not because they are finished, but be-

THE ASSISTANT

cause they are empty, and she believes they are empty because she is not living a life of epic emotional suffering.

Frank reads biographies of worldly successes like Napoleon and dreams of conquering the world like his heroes. The difference between Frank and Helen is that Frank is able to escape his idealism by living his life as it comes. He discovers that he does become a hero of sorts in emulating the worldly fool, St. Francis, and an even bigger fool, Morris Bober.

Frank's love for Helen also follows another medieval archetype. The medieval *Romance of the Rose* tells of a lover who receives one kiss from a rose and then spends the rest of the romance pursuing his unattainable love. This model is followed closely in the story that Frank tells Helen of his only love before her. Frank was in love with a carnival girl who died in an automobile accident after their affair had gone no farther than a single kiss. In this story, which foreshadows the romance of Frank and Helen, the carnival girl, though suggesting easy promiscuity, is a symbol pointing in the other direction. A carnival, like the Mardi Gras, originally marked the beginning of the Lenten season and in Latin meant "a farewell to the flesh." At first, Frank lusts after Helen, but his love soon idealizes her, first as a flower and then, more specifically, as a rose.

After forcing himself upon Helen, Frank tries to win her forgiveness by carving her a wooden bird and a wooden rose. She accepts only the rose, but when she finds out Frank's part in the robbery of her father's store, she throws the wooden rose in the trash. The rose becomes a symbol of Frank's death and rebirth when he falls into Bober's grave trying to see what Helen has thrown into it. When he recovers the rose, he feels the possibility of a new life and a new kind of love with Helen. At the end of the novel, Frank dreams that St. Francis has turned his wooden rose into a living one, suggesting his love for Helen has overcome its rigid idealism. Since it remains a rose, and a gift of the saint, Frank has perhaps turned his love into a higher ideal than the lustful romanticism of his first yearnings.

This spirit of transcendance illuminates both of the principals in Malamud's outwardly depressing tale. The store is many times called a prison, and Frank's wretched living quarters are seen as a cell. As Frank begins to take on the virtues of Bober, the cell becomes a place of monastic illumination. Each act of suffering for Bober and the rest of mankind strips away Frank's worldliness so that his act of becoming a Jew is, in St. Francis's terms, true *imitatio Christi*. Frank, who entered the novel as an orphan, has found a father; he was a drifter and has found a home; he cared about nothing and has found a love. Ward Minogue's curse "you filthy kike" has become a blessing as he has learned to love all the wretched of the earth.

Though Frank and his goodness survive past the end of the novel, he could have achieved nothing except by imitating Morris. Bober's goodness is seen through his little acts of kindness as well as in his suffering for Frank. As Frank, without Morris, could have ended up like Ward Minogue, so Morris could have ended up like two wretched Jews who wander through the novel, Breitbart, a light bulb salesman, and Marcus, a cancer-riddled paper bag peddler. They are men without hope, but Bober cares about them, and when he visits Breitbart, he leaves a present for his son, even though he has nothing himself. Morris's feeding by giving credit to the poor becomes a metaphor for taking care of mankind, and his little neighborhood seems to be a community of nations with its Swedes, Norwegians, Poles, Germans, Italians, Irish, and Jews. Though often his customers avoid his shop for cheaper prices somewhere else, they are all aware of him as the moral center of their universe and buy a little from him to assuage their guilt at choosing the world rather than its goodness. Such is the way of the world, but Malamud's humble heroes shine beyond it.

CHAPTER FOUR

A NEW LIFE

T he academic satire in Malamud's third novel, *A New Life* (1961), is based on Malamud's experiences as an instructor at Oregon State University, where he taught from 1949 to 1961. Though the similarity of S. Levin, the novel's hero, to Malamud is problematical, Levin is the archetypal Malamudian hero. He is an outsider in every way—a city-bred easterner in a small western town, a Jew among gentiles (though little is made of this), a humanist in a school that lost its liberal arts after World War I. Despite a motto of Benjamin Franklin's over the chairman's desk welcoming strangers, Levin never fits in.

From almost the moment Levin arrives at Cascadia College, Levin finds much to criticize in the English Department. In particular, he is appalled by the absence of humanities in the Humanities Building. In the department, literature is ignored for the teaching of grammar, a study whose bible is the chairman's text, *The Elements of Grammar* (now in its thirteenth edition). Even the composition course has as its reader *Science in Technology*. The chairman is proud of his anti–liberal

A NEW LIFE

arts department, of its freedom from genius of any kind, and of its lack of pressure to publish. The chairman, Orville Fairchild, thinks of Roosevelt as a Communist and is especially pleased to have canceled a class order for *The Communist Manifesto*. The Manifesto had been ordered by Leo Duffy, a "disagreeable radical," who has since been fired. Fairchild is a native of Moscow, Idaho, and he seems to be reacting to this accident of fate. Levin in his newly assigned position as chairman of the textbook committee will quickly find himself opposed to the textbooks and the principles of the Cascadia English Department. And this will not be enough: he will try to move from being a supporter of the humanities to being a champion of humanity.

Levin has moved west to start a new life, to get over his alcoholism, and to find himself. At first, Levin is merely a fool. He falls into every trap nature and society can set for him. He wets his pants twice on his first meeting with Gilley; he steps in a cow flop; he delivers his first lecture with his fly open. This foolishness is exaggerated as Levin tries to become part of the western culture of Cascadia.

When the New Yorker arrives in Easchester, the town in which Cascadia is located, he brings mythic preconceptions of the west. He expects the frontier virtues of freedom, independence, courage, and accord with nature. One by one these expectations are shattered. Instead of freedom, he finds a moral code that could not be more antithetical to the notion of the Wild West: beards do not fit (he has one), drinking is discouraged (he was an alcoholic) because the chairman's wife is a member of the Anti-Liquor League, and all sexual behavior outside of marriage is condemned (he is the only young bachelor in the department).

Instead of rugged individualism, he finds that his colleagues teach so that their students can pass the departmental objective grammar test, that they accept, not merely the chairman's outdated text, but even his ancient political views. Everywhere Levin finds cowardice where he expected courage. Even the love of nature Levin expects of the west is nothing more than an avocation. Though several members of the department are avid fishermen, they see their university as one that will teach men to fell trees, dam rivers, and run highways over mountains. Flycasting has become a course in which students are graded. The forest that dominates the first part of the novel turns out to be no wilderness at all, but a preserve of the forestry school. There is nothing wild in the west of Easchester.

Levin's struggle for humane values is ultimately conducted against the two men who are expected to vie for the chairmanship on the anticipated retirement of Fairchild, C. D. Fabrikant and Gerald Gilley. Levin immediately finds a western appeal in Fabrikant, the man recognized as the department's only scholar. Though Harvard-educated, Fabrikant seems to have some of the orneriness associated with old men in the west. He steers clear of departmental politics, scorns the rest of his colleagues, and is on horseback when Levin first meets him. As Levin sees the weakness in the rest of the department

A NEW LIFE

he turns to Fabrikant as his hero, and eventually becomes the leader of the pro-Fabrikant forces. Despite his stated contempt for departmental politics, Fabrikant, an associate professor, keeps putting off declaring for chairman in order to protect his possible promotion. Levin goes out on a limb for Fabrikant, and then Fabrikant saws it off.

Levin's prime antagonist is Gerald Gilley, the Director of Composition. Gilley, a photographer, always deals with life at at least one remove. He is constantly taking pictures of events instead of participating in them, and his academic pursuit is a picture history of American Literature, largely based on pictures cut out of *Life* magazine (life at three removes). Though a florid picture of health, Gilley is physically, as well as spiritually, sterile. He is, unlike Fabrikant, a man of hearty good cheer, and Levin will find it hard to undermine his chamber-of-commerce smiles and his "all for the good of Cascadia" boosterism.

Malamud reserves a good deal of irony for his hero. Levin makes idealistic resolutions about how he will stand up for freedom immediately after he has backed down to Gilley over censorship of a rather innocent story, Hemingway's "Ten Little Indians." Malamud uses setting to undermine Levin's idealism. Levin is standing in front of a urinal in the men's room, listening through the wall to Fabrikant lecture on Emerson. Though Fabrikant's dry voice hardly conjures up Emerson's spirit of nonconformism, Levin gets carried away and starts to footnote the lecture with citations from Chekhov and Richard Chase on the pursuit of freedom. Levin gets so excited that he bows to the urinal as if it were a crowd cheering his thoughts.

The scene looms large in relation to the McCarthyism that echoes through the novel. How many men were heroes to their mirrors—or urinals—and backed down when faced with the power of institutions that they privately despised? Levin will have to do a better job standing up to Cascadia than he has done in failing to defend Hemingway against Gilley.

Levin's road to moral perfection is not an easy one. He falls in love frequently and with great awkwardness, each time misusing some part of the western setting. He begins in classic comic fashion by botching an attempt to culminate, in a barn, an affair with a waitress. The rendezvous loses all its bucolic charm, even before it is interrupted by a mad Syrian. Levin is surprised to find out that only horses and not cows use blankets. When Levin, thinking of the Song of Songs, tells the girl her breasts smell like hay, she is offended and replies that she always bathes. Finally, Levin, barefoot and half-naked, walks back to town raising blisters and cutting his feet, while the girl, more comfortable with her shoes off, curses his failed manhood. Levin is no country boy, but he is not ready to give up trying.

Levin's affair with a student starts out more promisingly, as the mythic stakes are increased from bucolic tryst to voyage of exploration. The girl arranges to meet Levin at an aunt's motel on the Pacific Coast, and his desperate journey there in a "new" used car (he has just learned to drive) is meant to rival

A NEW LIFE

Balboa's discovery of the Pacific. After a number of comic disasters, Levin reaches the Pacific and the girl, and experiences a temporary moment of triumph.

This affair founders on a moral issue, which is less sexual than academic. The girl, Nadalee Hammerschmidt, gets angry with Levin when he refuses to raise her grade on an exam. Though he has violated a basic code in sleeping with the girl, he becomes a man of principle in refusing to bend on the matter of grades. Since Levin has only contempt for the exam in question, his moral rigidity seems overdone. Here Levin treats matters of morality too neatly, thinking he can separate the sexual issue from the academic one, even though both involve the same girl. When Levin discovers that Nadalee's grade should be raised because of an arithmetical error, he is able to change the grade without compromising his principles. He smugly congratulates himself on his rectitude, but does not guess that the fates will not let him get away so easily next time. In his next sexual affair, he will learn that it is not so easy to compartmentalize morality.

It does not take long for Levin to realize that his affair with Nadalee Hammerschmidt will not satisfy his desire to start a new life, to go beyond learning how to live and on to living. After a fall and winter of nonproductive academic and sexual life, Levin finds new hope in the spring. While bird-watching (the book, like all of Malamud's early work, is full of bird and flower images) in the woods, with visions of Daniel Boone in his head, Levin meets and makes love to Pauline Gilley, the wife of his immediate superior. The scene is one of never-to-be-repeated sylvan splendor, marred only slightly by the fact that the forest belongs to the forestry school.

Levin's affair with Pauline Gilley is vital to him because it validates his move west as the beginning of a new life. Pauline prevents his return to his old life when she appears at his door just at the moment he is about to fall off the wagon. Her presence enables him to resist the desire to take a drink. Pauline carries with her the familiar Malamudian symbols of fruitfulness and fertility—lemons, oranges, and the smell of flowers. She reveals that her children are adopted, and therefore, despite her fruitfulness, her maternal instincts have not been fulfilled.

The wooing of Pauline Gilley follows in rough outline the wooing of Beatrice in Dante's *Vita Nuova*. As Dante tells the story of his growing love for Beatrice, he reveals how he has to get through a number of masks (*schermi*) and images (*simulacra*) of Beatrice before he can reach a full perception of her nature. In the process of unveiling the true Beatrice, Dante makes a holy thing of his beloved. Levin has to go through a similar unmasking to reach the essential Pauline. After her appearance through the glass door, Levin meets Pauline in a rock garden during a party at a colleague's house. She is wearing a veil, which lends her an air of mystery. She reveals that her childlessness has been caused by her husband's infertility, not her own. At this point her desire for Levin is largely the statement of a biological need, and his desire for her is largely the product of her unattainability, symbolized by the veil and made real by her situation as his superior's wife.

A NEW LIFE

The limited rock garden is replaced temporarily by the openness of the forest where the sexual part of their love is consummated, and Levin's longing is brought to an end. Longing, a combination of sexual desire and the need to replace loneliness with companionship, is a common plaint of Malamud's heroes. It responds temporarily to sexual fulfillment, but needs love to be permanently vanquished.

After the forest idyll, the universe of Levin and Pauline is reduced to Levin's double bed in a rented room. It is not enough for either of them. Levin, whose name suggests his priestly function, is overwhelmed by guilt to the point that he suffers terrible rectal pain "like a rooster trying to lay an egg." The guilt is not for the affair, but for his refusal to allow himself to love. When this knot of "love ungiven" is broken, the pain disappears. Levin finds that he has given value to his life through love. He sees the power of love in its ability to "perfect each imperfect thing."

In Malamud's novels, the hero struggles to achieve love, but he struggles even more to reject love. If pain and longing validate love, so the sacrifice of giving it up sanctifies it. Milton's great work is *Paradise Lost*, for only in the loss can the paradise, for Levin a bright day in a university forest, be measured. Levin accepts a newer, deeper loneliness in rejecting Pauline so that both can go on with their lives. He has fallen in love with Pauline because he is a moral man, and he must reject her for the same reason. He discovers that he must oppose the policies of Gilley, and he can do that only if he is personally a moral man. He cannot condemn Gilley's immorality in cen-

A NEW LIFE

Levin, though terribly disappointed in his students, does not accept the impossibility of the task before him. He begins to care about his students' lives, urges them to put a foundation of humanity under their technical education, and—horror of horrors—counsels a few of them to go to the other state university. Finally appalled by both choices, Gilley and Fabrikant, Levin imagines the unimaginable: Levin as chairman. He pursues this quest with a fervor the Humanities Building has never seen and draws to himself a number of secret converts. They remain secret to the end, however, and in the election, right before he is fired, Levin garners not a single vote. He does accomplish something in his Quixotic campaign: a more humanities-oriented reader is substituted in most of the composition courses.

Levin sees a glimpse of the future he will not be allowed to follow when he becomes a witness to the death of Fairchild, the current chairman. The last words on Fairchild's lips seem pregnant with meaning as he stammers, "the mystery of the infin . . ." and Levin offers "infinite." Fairchild manages to gasp out the last word, and the mind of a man who has dedicated his life to a grammar text is exposed. What Fairchild has pondered all his life is the mystery of the infinitive. Hamlet's eternal question is reduced from a consideration of existence and annihilation to a problem of grammar.

Levin tries to escape from all this pettiness by returning to nature, particularly, birdwatching. Birds usually present a positive image in Malamud. Here, as in *The Assistant*, the hero sees his beloved as a bird, so it is not surprising that Levin

A NEW LIFE

Levin, though terribly disappointed in his students, does not accept the impossibility of the task before him. He begins to care about his students' lives, urges them to put a foundation of humanity under their technical education, and—horror of horrors—counsels a few of them to go to the other state university. Finally appalled by both choices, Gilley and Fabrikant, Levin imagines the unimaginable: Levin as chairman. He pursues this quest with a fervor the Humanities Building has never seen and draws to himself a number of secret converts. They remain secret to the end, however, and in the election, right before he is fired, Levin garners not a single vote. He does accomplish something in his Quixotic campaign: a more humanities-oriented reader is substituted in most of the composition courses.

Levin sees a glimpse of the future he will not be allowed to follow when he becomes a witness to the death of Fairchild, the current chairman. The last words on Fairchild's lips seem pregnant with meaning as he stammers, "the mystery of the infin . . ." and Levin offers "infinite." Fairchild manages to gasp out the last word, and the mind of a man who has dedicated his life to a grammar text is exposed. What Fairchild has pondered all his life is the mystery of the infinitive. Hamlet's eternal question is reduced from a consideration of existence and annihilation to a problem of grammar.

Levin tries to escape from all this pettiness by returning to nature, particularly, birdwatching. Birds usually present a positive image in Malamud. Here, as in *The Assistant*, the hero sees his beloved as a bird, so it is not surprising that Levin finds Pauline in the woods when he is out birdwatching. Birds in this aspect are associated with freedom of the spirit and emotion as they are in Keats's "To a Nightingale." For Malamud's souls trapped in the pettiness of daily life, the heart soaring like a bird is the image of the freedom love can bring.

Loss of birds, on the other hand, usually has a negative connotation. When Levin decides that he must break off his romance, his landlady's cat brings him dead birds, signs of his dead love. This imagery is reflected in the names of characters as well. An apparently plagiarized paper is turned in by a student named Albert O. Birdless. The attempt to prove that the work is plagiarism turns out, ironically, to be the only activity at Cascadia College that resembles scholarship or faculty cooperation. During the search for the plagiarism, no one objects when Levin spends weeks in the library tracking down the citation instead of grading objective exams. Eventually, other faculty members, including Gilley and Avis Fliss, join in the hunt, and the ideas in the Birdless paper are the only ones ever mentioned by the faculty of Cascadia. Through it all they are haunted by the slowly yellowing figure of Birdless, who is watching the fruitless search with smirking despair.

Another negative character with a bird name is Avis Fliss. No *rara avis*, she turns out to be, like Memo in *The Natural*, a woman with a sick breast, though her eyes flutter like "birds' wings." She and Levin try to seduce each other in his office by reading poetry from an anthology, but the seduction fizzles as she continues to talk about her benign tumor. Avis, who will turn out to be the "company" spy, is the only woman who objects to Levin's whiskers and urges that he become beardless.

Malamud punningly connects the two conditions of beardlessness and birdlessness so that Levin cuts off his beard almost at the time that the cat brings him the dead birds. Levin's beard (anathema to Cascadia, though attractive to the women in his life, except Avis) is a symbol of his birdlike freedom. He snips it off after watching with his binoculars Pauline and Gerald Gilley reunited at a basketball game. The cutting of the beard is done out of grief at his lover's reunion with her husband and guilt (one of the students identifies her bearded professor as an adulterer). The binoculars are part of a pattern of images of lenses and windows. Levin's birdwatching binoculars are a sign of his capability to see things clearly, at long range, and in perspective. One of his students even jokes that they may have x-ray powers, foreshadowing Levin's ability to see clearly into moral issues. Levin's adversary, Gilley, uses the camera as his primary tool, evidencing his preference for images of life rather than life itself.

The weakness of the novel lies in the unconvincing moral issues that lead to Levin's firing. There are two, both involving pieces of paper. The first is a list of those professors athletes should avoid, a list kept by George Bullock, member of the department and the athletes' tutor. Such a list, in the context of McCarthyite blacklisting, might cause some outrage among more delicate moral sensibilities, but for Levin to expect action in philistine Cascadia is foolish. Though Gilley's rationalizing along the lines that athletes are people too has some comic quality, the defense of the list seems unnecessary. Furthermore, Levin seems in as much of a snit because his name is on the list as for any higher principle.

The second issue involves a photograph taken by Gilley of his wife and Duffy swimming in the nude. The revelation of this photo caused C. D. Fabrikant to give up local faculty support for the protection of Duffy's rights after he was improperly fired for intellectual troublemaking. Levin makes an issue of the presumption of adultery from the fact of the nudity. This argument might hold in court of law and has some resonance because of guilt by association techniques in the McCarthy era, but the point is far too subtle for Cascadia. Levin's insistence on this distinction almost completely clouds the issue of whether Duffy had the right to fair dismissal procedures even if he was sleeping with Pauline, that is, does a man with obnoxious personal morals have the same rights as one with morals agreeable to the community. Perhaps Levin's obsession with the peripheral issue comes from his shaky footing in the personal morals department. It is hard for Levin to be objective on the Duffy affair since Levin had been taking "obnoxious" intellectual stands while sleeping with Pauline.

Gilley, when he finally discovers the affair, turns the tables on Levin. As the price for allowing Levin to go off with the pregnant (by Levin) Pauline, Gilley gets Levin to swear never to become a college teacher again (he may, if he wants, teach high school). Levin, although he is not certain he still loves Pauline—at least some of the original fires are out—agrees to the bargain. What Gilley has offered Levin is a clas-

A NEW LIFE

sic dilemma in choosing between love and honor—only here neither of the alternatives has the proper weight. Despite Levin's theoretical love of college teaching, his year at Cascadia has offered him little or no pleasure or reward, not even the proverbial student brought up from philistine darkness. Furthermore, it is unlikely that Levin, who got this job only because Pauline liked his picture on the application, would get another job. Perhaps Gilley is clever enough to see that forbidding college teaching to Levin will make him miserable because of the prohibition. On the other hand, the option of rescuing Pauline is tainted by the fact that Gilley still loves her, would take her back, and is financially in a position to raise a family of five. Perhaps this is the *schlemiehl's* dilemma: to be troubled by a choice between giving up a career he doesn't want and rescuing a woman he doesn't love who probably would be better off unrescued. This happens all the time to traditional *schlemiehls* like I. B. Singer's Gimpel where the point is Gimpel's innocent choice of the holiness of love over all the moral judgments of others. Usually when Malamud gives us this choice, as when Bok in *The Fixer* acknowledges "his" child or Frank Alpine stays with the failing grocery in *The Assistant*, the alternative has been given value by the actions of the hero. In *A New Life*, the love value to some extent has been validated by Levin's devotion, but the career value has been undermined by the satire.

CHAPTER FIVE

THE FIXER

At first glance, Malamud's fixer, Yakov Bok, seems to be a victim. His name, Bok ("goat" in German) suggests the scapegoat he does become in a government plot to charge the Jews of Russia with the ritual murder of a Christian child. Bok's name, however, also suggests another goat, the one kid of the song *chad gad-yah*, which is sung at the end of the Passover Seder. The song tells of a single kid which has been devoured by a cat. Each of a series of destructive forces—dog, stick, fire, water, ox, and butcher—annihilates the one before it until the Angel of Death takes the butcher. Then the Most Holy destroys the Angel of Death and only He—and, surprisingly, the one kid—remain. The song symbolizes the survival of the Jewish people while all the nations who have persecuted it have perished. Malamud, at the end of the novel, does not tell us the outcome of Bok's trial, but there is no question about the fate of the government that persecuted him. The novel begins in the spring of 1911 and ends in the winter of 1913. The death knell for Tsarist Russia, Bok's perse-

THE FIXER

cutor, has already been sounded. By 1917, the Tsar will abdicate, ending a thousand years of merciless monarchy.

The Fixer (1966) is an examination of freedom and its complement, commitment. Yakov Bok, the title character, spends most of the novel in prison, and, paradoxically, the longer he is imprisoned the more true freedom he attains. Malamud starts his hero off with the appearance of a good deal of freedom. Much of it comes from having no responsibility, no so-called "hostages to fortune." His parents are dead; his wife has left him; he has no children; his job requires only his bag of tools; he has no financial obligations; and his religion means nothing to him.

Free of the restraint of commitment, the fixer sets off to see the world. He leaves the world of the *shtetl* behind when a boatman, resembling Charon, the Ferryman of Hell, carries him across the Dnieper River. When the boatman makes an anti-Semitic speech, Bok throws the bag containing his prayer shawl overboard, signifying the abandonment of his religion. For the first third of the novel, Bok will strip himself of his identity as a Jew. He has already shaved his beard. He will change his name, deny his religion, and live among Christians. Then when Bok, in the last two-thirds of the novel, gradually reassumes his identity as a Jew, it will be a completely willed act, that is, Bok will be a Jew because he chooses rather than because he was born one.

Like most of Malamud's heroes, Bok takes himself almost immediately into the enemy camp. When he gets to Kiev (Russia's Christian Holy City), he stays briefly in the Jewish quarter, but a chance occurrence puts him into the Christian sector that is forbidden to Jews. He rescues a wealthy drunk who has fallen in the snow. The man, Lebedev, turns out to be a member of the Black Hundred, an anti-Semitic organization. Since he does not know that his clean-shaven rescuer is a Jew, Lebedev invites Bok to stay on his property. From this act of charity, Bok's troubles begin.

Bok sees his rescue of Lebedev as the beginning of the good fortune he has left the ghetto of Kiev to find. He does not, of course, know that in Malamud's novels any apparent good luck leads invariably to disaster. When Lebedev offers him a job at a fantastic wage and then a position as an overseer, Bok seems to have found his luck, and he congratulates himself on his good fortune. This good luck seems doubled, when Lebedev's daughter, Zinaida, offers him her sexual favors. Like all the temptresses in Malamud who have no love to accompany their sexual desire, Zinaida is slightly crippled. Bok is ready to submit to her temptations, until he discovers that she is having her period. In Jewish Law, this makes her unclean, and Bok, though believing he has left all that behind, rejects her. Despite his description of himself as a free-thinker, he will learn that his heritage is much harder to give up than he believes.

When a Christian boy is murdered by his mother's lover, the Russian authorities raise the specter of ritual murder (i.e., Jews murdering Christian children so that their blood can be used for making matzos) in order to deflect criticism of a regime whose public policies, especially the disastrous Russo-

THE FIXER

Japanese War of 1905, had led to a demand for loosening repressive conditions. In particular, there was agitation to end the Pale of Settlement, a small strip of Russia near the Polish border in which most Jews were restricted. A conviction for ritual murder would be enough to turn the tide against a more liberal policy. Though Bok knows nothing about these forces until near the end of his imprisonment, this insignificant man becomes a focal point in Russian history.

Nowhere is Malamud so relentless in stripping away all the props a man has to defend himself against the demons of fear, loneliness, and even madness. This is done in two stages. First, Yakov is systematically deprived of human society and the consequent ability to depend upon it for help, for companionship, and for self-definition. Once this external support is removed, the authorities attempt to undermine Bok's inner resources.

When he enters the prison population, Bok appears to gain important human support. By passing the test of not informing, he gains a few friends among the prisoners. Then he meets a fellow Jew, a counterfeiter named Gronfein, who promises to get his story to the Jewish population. Finally, he finds the Investigating Magistrate—though not the prosecutor—on his side. In each case, Bok depends on others and is disappointed. When Gronfein (he *is* an informer) betrays him to the prison authorities, Bok is removed from the general prison population and put into solitary confinement. Bok places all his hope in Bibikov, an honest man who is the Investigating Magistrate.

UNDERSTANDING BERNARD MALAMUD

Bibikov knows, but cannot yet prove, that Marfa Golov, the mother of the murdered child, and Marfa's lover are responsible for the child's death. For almost half the novel, Bok waits for Bibikov to find the evidence to incriminate Marfa, but then in an apparent act of carelessness, Bok's guard leaves his cell open. In this novel, any surface freedom is deceiving. Bok sneaks out of his cell and gets far enough to see the prisoner in the next cell. It is Bibikov, who has hanged himself after being arrested for his interference in the government's prosecution of Bok. Bibikov is the just man in a corrupt system. He cracks under pressure put on him, ironically by the Minister of Justice, to manufacture evidence of Bok's guilt. Though Bibikov does not betray Bok, he fails him.

Bibikov does not understand that it is not enough to know the truth, one must be committed to it totally. Bibikov's weakness is seen early in the novel when he discusses Spinoza with Bok. Bibikov is kind, yet patronizing, in discussing the Jewish philosopher with his less well-educated prisoner, but he is much further from the essence of Spinoza than Bok. Bibikov uses Spinoza to rationalize his political position of serving a regime whose principles appall him. He misunderstands Spinoza's notion of conditional freedom and uses him as a model of political cooperation. "He also thought man was freer when he participated in the life of society than when he lived in solitude as he himself did. He thought that a free man in society had a positive interest in promoting the happiness and intellectual emancipation of his neighbors." When Bibikov finds he can no longer serve both his government and his con-

THE FIXER

science he hangs himself. His broken glasses lie on the cell floor indicating the blindness of the intellectual. Bok will come to understand Spinoza's idea of freedom.

Bibikov's death temporarily crushes Bok. He returns to his cell without hope. After all, if Bibikov with his resources of intelligence, honesty, and even a small amount of authority, can do nothing for Bok or for himself, what can Bok do?

The death of Bibikov marks a new phase of Bok's life. His legs become gangrenous, and he is forced to crawl to the infirmary for treatment. This act is seen as near martyrdom by the other prisoners, and their scorn of the Jew turns to such admiration that one prisoner risks death to bind Bok's wounds. When Bok returns from the infirmary, he is put in a new cell, the season changes from autumn to winter, and he is reminded that any attempt to escape or to attack the prison officials will result in immediate execution. At first this ruling is a threat, but the quick death it promises becomes a temptation to be overcome.

This phase of the novel is presided over by Warden Grizitskoy and focuses on the attempt, through physical deprivation, to get Bok to confess. Bok is poisoned, strip-searched, chained, near-frozen, with no lasting effect except to focus his energies against his captors. It is in this phase that the government's refusal to indict him becomes an issue. Ultimately, Bok is kept in prison for two years with no indictment. Without an indictment, not only is he not permitted a lawyer, but also all temporal reference is removed. As he notes, if he had been sentenced to twenty years in Siberia, two years would have some meaning. Without an indictment, time itself becomes meaningless. The refusal of the government to indict is part of a pattern that removes all tokens by which Bok can give his life order. His captors will not tell him what day it is nor when he can expect his indictment. For a while, Bok uses the cleaning of his cell, particularly sweeping, as something to do, something to give every day some shape. Bok struggles against the formlessness of his life in prison. He uses broomstraws to mark days, weeks, and months, even though he has no exact starting date. Eventually his broom wears out and is not replaced.

The test for Bok is to see if he can build some semblance of order out of nothing but his mind. It is in this sense, that the novel's title gets its significance. As a fixer, as opposed, let's say, to his father-in-law, Shmuel the peddler, Bok has no stock-in-trade except his own skill. Out of the fragments of his memories and out of his growing conviction, he must shape his life. In this effort, he becomes like his intellectual hero, Baruch Spinoza, the Dutch philosopher, who was scorned by his fellow Jews, even as he imagined a freedom beyond anything they could conceive. Bok is far too modest to compare himself to Spinoza, but his achievement of interior freedom rivals that of the philosopher.

Bok builds his life out of principle, but also out of his suffering. At the beginning of the novel, he wonders why God would let his Chosen People suffer the way the Jews have had to suffer throughout history. Such doubts lead him to agnosticism. What Bok learns is that suffering in fact builds charac-

THE FIXER

ter. At the end of the novel, as the government becomes desperate for his confession, he is offered all sorts of compromises that he clearly would have accepted at the beginning of his imprisonment. The price he has already paid in suffering makes it impossible to compromise, and at that point, though he doesn't know it, he has the government at his mercy, rather than vice versa.

Though Bok considers himself a nobody, and even something of a coward, he proceeds to win a number of small triumphs, that culminate in a major victory. His first triumph comes after he has been poisoned by the prison officials, who hope that the poisoning will weaken him enough so that he will confess. At this point, Bok realizes that he can bargain with his life. If he is not afraid to die, he can begin to control his fate. After the poisoning, he refuses to eat unless he is permitted to eat with the rest of the prison population. When a starving man has the courage to fast, his enemies have lost one weapon that they can use against him.

Though Bok declines physically throughout the novel, he rapidly gains a moral strength that overwhelms his captors. Both the Prison Warden and Grubeshov, the Prosecuting Attorney, grow more and more nervous as they are unable to deal with the fixer's persistence. Grubeshov, in particular, begins to decay as he is unable to get Bok to confess. He has based his political career on what had once seemed a rather simple matter, but two years into Bok's imprisonment without indictment, Grubeshov begins by offering compromises and ends by ranting and raving at the fixer. Grubeshov threatens

Bok by noting that the Tsar has taken a personal, negative interest in the case, by warning that a failure to confess will result in massive pogroms against the Jews. He even offers Bok safe passage out of the country if he will confess. These pressures strengthen instead of weaken Bok as he learns how important he is to the state at large and to his people in particular. More than anything Bok matters.

For Malamud, suffering is more than a test or a measure; it is life itself, particularly the life of the Jews throughout history. They have a convenant with their God, and, in the nature of all such one-sided agreements, they break the rules and pay for their transgressions. To know the rules, to try to keep them, to break the rules, and to pay for breaking them is human experience. Its rigor separates the Jews from the rest of mankind and, in fact, gives them a vitality lacking in God himself. God can do almost anything except suffer like a man.

This is no abstract notion to Malamud, and he shows that Bok's ability to learn from his suffering distinguishes him from the Tsar. The murder of Zhenia Golov (in which the body is drained of blood) is misused by the Tsar to further his political ends, even though he of all people, as the father of a haemophiliac, should try to use love rather than hate in dealing with a child's body that has lost all its blood. At the end of the novel, Bok has a dream-conversation with Tsar Nicholas II in which the Tsar refuses to learn the converse of suffering, mercy. In the scheme of things, mercy is most meaningful when practiced by those who have suffered the most, and presumably have the least to give. Bok asks the Tsar, as someone

THE FIXER

who has suffered and needs mercy himself, to be merciful. The Tsar refuses to accept responsibility for the pogroms that might arise from the ritual murder charges, pleading that he is helpless to stem the tide of history. By this time Bok knows too much of the nature of history to accept this evasion. He knows that if even a lowly fixer can change history, so can the Tsar. For this refusal to have mercy, Bok (in the dream) shoots the Tsar, much the way the Old Testament God punished Israel for its violations of its covenant.

Bok does better than the Tsar when it comes to learning from suffering. He is tested when his indictment is delivered by Raisl, the wife who had betrayed him and had run off with another man. She has come to ask a favor of the man she deserted, now a half-starved wretch who has been imprisoned for two years. One would think Bok would be in no position to grant favors of any kind. Raisl has come to beg Bok to give his name to her illegitimate child. Though Bok had cursed her treachery and could feel justified in turning his back on her, he instead claims the child as his own (in writing on the envelope which contains his indictment). At the same time he denies the charges in the indictment and boldly scrawls his innocence across the papers where the signature of his confession is expected.

After this climactic scene, Bok seems in control of the situation, though he still is tempted from his principles. A priest is sent to offer him a share in a general pardon being issued by the Tsar. Bok could accept the pardon without asking any questions and walk out of prison a "free man," but he is sharp enough to realize that accepting a pardon would assume his guilt. When he verifies this with the priest, Bok refuses to accept the pardon. The priest calls him a fool for being such a stickler for the letter of the law, but Bok has clearly acted on principle.

Bok finally gives himself the ultimate freedom when he rejects suicide as an alternative and chooses to live. Since his only possible suicide weapon (a needle for slitting his wrists) has been taken from him, Bok has only one means of suicide left—provoking the Russians into shooting him. His refusal to entertain this option takes away his last external freedom because he had always been able to tell himself that if things got bad enough he could strike a guard or the warden and be free from his suffering. Such an act would even have the added attraction of looking like courage, though it would be a desperation that would make all his previous suffering meaningless. At this point, when Bok understands that removing a choice increases his freedom, he has achieved the freedom defined by his hero Spinoza. For Spinoza, freedom lies not in choice of action, but in full understanding of the implications of one's decisions. Once the fixer chooses life, no one can impose his will upon him. The Russians can kill him if they want, but they can no longer get him to provoke them into killing him.

Just as he has to come to terms with his freedom, so Bok also has to come to terms with his Jewishness. As always, Malamud is not content to say a man is a Jew because he is born a Jew. Bok clearly puts all that behind when he crosses the Dnie-

THE FIXER

per and enters Kiev, or so he thinks. When he rescues Lebedev, he ignores the Black Hundreds pin that marks the fallen man as an anti-Semite.

Bok thinks he has left behind more than just his religion. He thinks he can be a man with no politics and blithely tells Lebedev that he is not political, a statement fraught with naïveté in Russia at the turn of the century. Bok believes that being uncommitted in everything can keep him out of trouble, when in fact commitment will become his only way to exist. Just as he tells Lebedev he has no politics, so he tells Bibikov, the Investigating Magistrate, that he has no religion. There is something childlike in Bok's proclamation that he is a free-thinker. He wants to give the impression that he has a home-spun philosophy and is pleased when Bibikov makes more of his philosophical powers than is warranted. Here, too, his un-committedness turns against him. He discusses Spinoza with Bibikov, expanding on the former's notion of freedom with no sense that such abstract matters can have any bearing on his own life. He does not realize that both his life and his sanity will depend upon his being able to live Spinoza's dream of freedom.

Fortunately for Bok, he can never remain as uncommit-ted as he says he is. He gets involved with Lebedev, after briefly reflecting that touching the fallen man could get him into trouble. But there is a human being suffocating in the snow and he acts. He acts again against his own principles of non-commitment when he rescues an old Hasidic Jew from some boys and takes him in. Bok does not identify himself as a Jew, but he is touched when the old man takes out some matzos. Bok has lost so much of his roots that he does not even know it is Passover. Bok dreams about the Hasid, and in his dream it is he who is hiding (in the graveyard) and the Hasid finds *him*. In the dream, Bok hits the Hasid in the head with his hammer. He is angry with the Hasid because he has found the real Bok hiding from his emotions and his Jewishness. When the Hasid prays, Bok shuts his eyes because he does not want to be reminded of what he has left behind, and he hurries the old Jewish man out of his life.

As it turns out, the Russian authorities don't want him to forget his Jewishness either. It is to their purposes that Bok look like a Jew with long beard and earlocks, and so they refuse to let him cut his hair. After a while, they give him a prayer shawl and phylacteries. One of the guards urges him to sway like Jews do in the temple. Little by little Bok will look more and more like the old man he pushed out of his life.

Though the Russians are at first pleased with this transformation, they discover, much to their chagrin, that they cannot deal with Bok's change into a Jew. When one of the guards slips Bok a copy of the New Testament, Bok, to keep his mind sharp, begins to memorize the Beatitudes and to chant them aloud as if they were Jewish prayers. This convinces the authorities that Bok has weakened, and they send a priest to convert him. In fact, Bok has used the Beatitudes, with their message of the strength of the poor and the meek, to strengthen his own faith. Not only does he refuse conversion and the freedom it will bring, but also, he rises, wearing prayer

THE FIXER

shawl and phylacteries, out of the gloom of his cell, and appears to tower over the priest.

The New Testament and phylacteries are taken from him and his guard throws into his cell torn pages of the Old Testament (in Hebrew). This is meant as a gesture of contempt since Bok has to use such paper for toilet paper. Bok collects the pages and begins to create his own psalms and prayers out of the fragments. His strength continues to grow as he realizes that his capacity for suffering both in his own right and for others makes him a better Jew. He ceases to fear the state, though he is enraged that it requires the Jew as victim to embody all its weakness and corruption. He also knows that every nation that has employed the Jew as scapegoat has crumbled, and that this history is sung at the end of the Passover service in the story of the one kid who survived all its predators. As a goat, Bok is the Jewish nation that has survived, in spite, or rather because, of its suffering. To be a Jew is to understand the suffering that God puts into the lives of all men. This understanding leads to goodness that must take the form of *rachmones*, pity, for other men, for other Jews, even for oneself. Without it, the suffering is meaningless and goodness nonexistent.

CHAPTER SIX

PICTURES OF FIDELMAN
and THE TENANTS

T|he Italian setting of Malamud's picaresque novel
Pictures of Fidelman (1969) proves to be the hero's greatest ob-
stacle even as it is the source of his growth. The novel, com-
posed of three previously collected stories ("Last Mohican,"
"Still Life," "Naked Nude") and three new chapters, follows Fidelman's progress as he changes from Jewish-American art
student to Italian artisan. Fidelman declines in "morality" as
he grows in humanity.

The novel's episodic structure shows Fidelman at different stages in his career. In each chapter, Fidelman pursues a
different kind of artistic endeavor, lives (after two chapters in
Rome) in a different Italian city (Milan, Florence, Naples, and
Venice), and loses a different part of his American values. In
the landscape of Italy, vices and virtues have grown together
so long that they can no longer be separated one from the other.
Moral choices can still be made, but they are far more complex than they would be in America. Fidelman's Italy is a
world whose painters for 700 years have been using their most

sensual women for their Virgins, whose sculptors (e.g., Bernini in his Santa Teresa) make spiritual ecstasy (the soul leaving the body) look like sexual ecstasy, whose charlatans were creating false religious relics hundreds of years before Columbus set sail for America, and whose prostitutes served Crusaders on their way to the Holy Land. In such a world, vice and evil are not necessarily the same thing.

As Fidelman moves from city to city he associates with increasingly corrupt people. He shares a villa with a woman painter who has been her uncle's lover, then two thieves take him prisoner and make him into an art forger, and later he gets involved with a whore and her pimp. Fidelman declines even faster than his surroundings and progresses from forger to pimp to heroin user to homosexual. These changes do not make him worse, however, but rather teach him about art and life, often reversing rather idealistic notions he has—especially about art. Almost never do these lessons improve his art, but they tell him about the richness of life that inspires the great art of others. This, in turn, enriches his own life, even if he has little to show for living. Each chapter shows Fidelman ending rather than beginning some phase of his artistic life, yet the close of the novel is optimistic as it concludes that Fidelman has made a good beginning in both art and life.

The ancient civilization of Italy distinguishes this novel from all Malamud's other works. This civilization created art treasures so old they have become civilization itself and vices so ancient they seem bred into the blood. As Fidelman confronts this civilization, he is a naif, both childish and childlike, even though he is not portrayed as a young man after the first two chapters.

This naïveté allows him to respond to the richness of corruption that is taken for granted by the other characters. At some point in each chapter, Fidelman has a revelation that changes his perspective on his life and his art. Almost always this revelation is that he is more corrupt than he thinks, that he is weaker than he knows, and yet, that he is a man of much larger possibility than he had imagined. In this mind-expanding naïveté, he is like another Italian innocent, Dante, the poet's alter ego, who descended to Hell and was surprised at almost everything he found there. Malamud twice points out this allusion by having Fidelman refer to his Italian guides as Virgil, the classical poet who was Dante's guide through Hell and Purgatory.

Fidelman will stray far from the path usually tread by Malamud's heroes, but not in the first chapter, which is typical of Malamud—Jews finding Jews in the oddest of places and learning about responsibility and suffering. Fidelman, newly arrived in Rome, is accosted by Shimon Susskind, a *shnorrer* ("freeloader") and self-proclaimed guide, who demands charity of Fidelman, and what he wants is nothing less than one of Fidelman's two suits. Fidelman refuses, offers a reasonable gift instead, and subsequently finds himself haunted at every turn by the *shnorrer*. When Fidelman's first and only chapter of his book on Giotto disappears, he searches for Susskind through parts of Rome he never knew existed—a synagogue where Jews still mourn Italian victims of the Holocaust, a ghetto,

PICTURES OF FIDELMAN and THE TENANTS

and the Jewish cemetery where the gravestones mark the dead from Auschwitz. When Susskind is found selling cheap rosaries, he seems like nothing more than a con man, but Fidelman will find out different.

None of his adventure with the *shnorrer* makes any sense until Fidelman dreams of Susskind-Virgil emerging from a grave and leading Fidelman into a synagogue whose walls are adorned by a Giotto fresco showing St. Francis's charity. Then Fidelman understands that he cannot understand the history of Italian art until he understands the history of his own people, and he cannot understand Giotto until he understands the subjects he painted, that is, art is never separate from the life it represents. If he wants to know the meaning of Giotto's *St. Francis Giving His Robe to a Poor Man*, he has to give his suit to a poor man. Neither Auschwitz nor Giotto has anything to teach him if he doesn't learn this lesson. Fidelman delivers his suit to Susskind just in time to see him burning the last page of the missing chapter. This is the first of many times that his work will be destroyed because he has theory only, instead of the spirit that can be learned from experience.

The second Roman chapter, "Still Life," pursues the theme of the inextricable tangle of religion and life, though the religion is Catholicism in a chapter that is far more Italian in mood than the previous one. Fidelman's painting and his passion for a young woman painter are as dead as the Italian phrase for "still life," *natura morta*, until he costumes himself as a priest and arouses the woman's passion. Though Fidelman is surprised at this outcome, it should have been expected in a nation whose painters have exploited the similarities between religious passion and amorous passion and who understand how close the suffering for sin is to the pleasure of sinful sex. Fidelman discovers that there is *still life* in a relation he thought was dead.

In the third of the previously collected chapters, "Naked Nude," Fidelman is no longer an outsider, though he still has something to learn from the Italians. His companions are no longer merely eccentric, but true denizens of the underworld, and though Fidelman is pressured to join them in the theft of a priceless art treasure, he is not merely their pawn. Fidelman has been trying unsuccessfully to paint a nude that has the spirit as well as the body of a woman. His associates use his gambling debts to force him to forge a copy of a Titian nude, but he is unsuccessful until he gives himself up to his lowest thoughts: first, that we are all thieves, that every artist has stolen from others; and second, that love is often most real when it is most perverse. In this case, a memory of peeping through a keyhole at his sister taking a bath opens his mind to all the nudes he has ever seen, including Titian's. With this knowledge, he is more than a match for his captors. He engineers a double switch, steals the painting himself and falls in love with it, though he knows it is his copy and not the real thing. This forgery is the closest Fidelman will come to a masterpiece.

In the second half of the novel, which is all new Fidelman material, Malamud's hero is no longer an innocent. Fidelman has been working for years on his masterpiece, but he can

PICTURES OF FIDELMAN and THE TENANTS

never bring himself to finish it. By now his Florentine neighbors call him maestro, as much for the wonderful wooden madonnas he carves for the tourist trade as for his unfinished painting, *Mother and Child*. He sees his woodcarving (he never regards it as sculpture) as a kind of artistic whoredom to pay for his supplies. While working on his masterpiece Fidelman takes up with a whore, Esmeralda, whose pimp is outraged that his livelihood has been taken away. The pimp is, however, something of a romantic and will not stand in the way of Fidelman and Esmeralda as long as it is a matter of love.

Fidelman will only allow that it might become love (a common response of Malamud's heroes who often contemplate falling in love instead of doing it), and the pimp resolves to keep an eye on Fidelman and his whore. Though Fidelman has lived in Italy long enough not to be put off by the fact that his mistress is a whore, he eventually equates the two whoredoms—his in art and hers of the flesh—and decides that it is as moral for her to peddle her body as it is for him to peddle his madonnas (her price is the same as the price for a wooden madonna). At this point, Fidelman becomes a pimp himself, and the original pimp takes his revenge.

Fidelman has at last finished his picture (no longer *Mother and Child*, but *Prostitute and Procurer*) and is ready to marry the whore, when the pimp, pushed out of his own profession, turns art critic. He suggests a small change in the painting and Fidelman, uncomfortable with his finished picture, goes back to it and ruins it. The whore attacks him with a knife, but Fidelman disarms her and wounds himself in the gut. Malamud is fascinated with the theme of the artist who cannot face finishing his masterpiece and will treat it at full length in his next novel *The Tenants*.

After a chapter in which Fidelman experiments with a series of modern styles of painting (while Malamud tries to match those styles with his prose), Malamud resolves the career of Fidelman in both art and love. Fidelman, now gray-haired, laments having wasted his life on dreams of artistic fulfillment and tries to overcome his frustration by having an affair with Margherita, the wife of Beppo, a glass blower and a homosexual. While Fidelman is carrying on the affair, Beppo teaches him his craft, which Fidelman finds more substantial than anything else he has ever attempted artistically. When Beppo catches Fidelman in bed with his wife, he rapes him and then becomes Fidelman's lover, the first true love of his life. Fidelman learns the glass-blower's trade, but gives up Beppo to save Margherita's limited, but not unsatisfactory, marriage. As a craftsman, instead of an artist, Fidelman can practice an art that is not separated from life, and, in his affair with Beppo, he has learned a love that accepts all flaws and imperfections. With this knowledge, Fidelman's Italian experience is over, and he returns to America where he works at his trade and loves both men and women.

The Tenants (1971) might be considered a ferocious version of *The Assistant* because in it two men of utterly dissimilar backgrounds inhabit a minimal space while they forge fearsome bonds of love and hate, until each finally becomes a version of the other. It also might be considered a double version of the "Pimp's Revenge" chapter in *Pictures of Fidelman*. In this version, each of two men struggles to complete his own work of art, eventually sacrifices the same girl on the altar of his art, and then finally destroys both the art and the life of the other.

The novel restates most of Malamud's themes about the relation of life to art, but despite two vividly drawn central characters, the parallels and oppositions between them are so neatly drawn that the book is more dissertation than novel.

Harry Lesser, an experienced writer with two critically praised minor novels to his credit, is working on his masterpiece, *The Promised End*, the ultimate self-reflective novel about a novelist unable to finish his novel. He has been at it for nine years, refining form rather than content, and his last name defines what has happened to him in the meantime: he has grown to be less of a man than he was when he started. He has cut himself off from life and has become the last tenant in a building which is slated to be demolished as soon as his lease runs out. Though he has gotten no closer to the end of his novel than his protagonist has, he insists that the apartment house is the only place he can write and refuses to give up his lease, a decision which is driving his landlord, Levenspiel, crazy. Though Levenspiel is mostly a comic presence, almost certainly, like Ginzburg in "Idiots First," he is also the Angel of Death, here reminding Lesser of how little time art really has to accomplish its goals.

Despite the threats and bribes of Levenspiel, Lesser might have gone on, contentedly not finishing his novel, but for the appearance of a squatter in the building—a second writer named Willie Spearmint. Spearmint appears to be the opposite of Lesser in all things. He is black, young, outgoing, vital, and his writing lacks form, but seems to have substance; while Lesser is white, middle-aged, friendless, almost moribund, and his writing is all form without substance.

Despite these contrasts, the two men are novelists and, therefore, brothers under their very different skin. Willie, in fact, becomes so obsessed with his work that he refuses to sleep with his girl, Irene Bell, for fear of draining his artistic juices. Eventually Lesser takes up with the girl (who is white and Jewish), but Irene is no better off having Lesser for a lover than she was with Willie since Lesser always chooses art before life. He is the kind of man who prefers imagining vividly the winter to looking out the window and seeing the snow; furthermore, his imagined world is more vivid than the real one. Lesser tells Irene that he will marry her as soon as he finishes his novel, which is to say never. When she finally gives him up, she leaves a note telling him that no novel is as important as she is.

Unfortunately, neither of the men agree about this, and the closest Lesser comes to marriage is when he imagines his novel ending with himself and Willie involved in a double wedding amidst a very Jewish-sounding African tribe. In this fictional marriage, Willie marries Irene and Lesser marries a black woman he has met in Harlem. Though the two quarrel over Lesser's taking Willie's girl, the great battle is over the artistic frustrations that each brings to the other's life. Lesser envies the immediacy of Spearmint's experience and his ability to put it in writing, though he guesses wrong when he tries to separate the autobiographical elements from the made-up ones in Spearmint's writing (at least Spearmint says so). But the novel plays endlessly with the themes of appearance and reality or art and illusion so that Spearmint's claims about what is real and what is imagined may be lies. Spearmint, on the other hand, finds that Lesser's lessons about form inhibit him to the point that he bangs his head against the wall in frustration. Lesser is both pleased and disturbed that he has caused Spearmint trouble. Lesser wants Spearmint to succeed, but not before he does, and that, certainly, will be never.

So close is the relationship of love and hate in this novel that when Levenspiel comes upon the two men almost killing each other, he takes them for homosexual lovers. Each is looking for the best in the other, but they are both incapable of communicating except through the written word. Each also comes to depend on the other so that when one is not working, the other cannot work. Lesser wants to reach out in love to confirm this bond with his fellow novelist, but when he allows reasonable doubts to silence him, the only remaining recourse is to end their relationship bound in hate. Spearmint tries to get rid of Lesser by burning his manuscript, and Lesser, in turn, takes an axe to Spearmint's antique typewriter, the sign of Spearmint's place as a writer. This leads to even greater vengeance, in an act of mutual destruction that suggests that

UNDERSTANDING BERNARD MALAMUD

both men are parts of what between them could be whole. Spearmint is the intuitive in life and art, the creative force that Nietzsche characterized as Dionysian. Lesser is the ordering principle, Nietzsche's Apollonian spirit that shapes chaos. Art cannot exist without both of these forces coexisting, but Lesser and Willie destroy each other's vital organ—Willie puts an ax in Lesser's brain, while Lesser castrates Willie.

Though the novel repeats many of Malamud's notions about the danger of allowing art to swallow up life, the theme is unconvincing because the quality of life outside the tenement is never vital enough to match the intensity with which both men work at their novels. As she is presented in the novel, Irene Bell does not have any convincing appeal for either of the men, and it is not surprising that they choose to bang on their typewriters instead of her (Malamud's pun). The novel is most interesting and alive when it examines the obsessiveness that writing becomes—an obsessiveness that is not necessarily dependent upon the talent of the writers involved. Lesser, in particular, shows how a novel can write its author rather than vice versa, how it can make demands not only on his time and his talent, but on his soul. Lesser also finds that the novel tends to write itself through him. It will not let him end it, for this would violate its premise that the end must always be promised. Furthermore, the novel knows that it will cease to live at the moment the last period is put in place. In order to create the novel as sentient thing, Malamud plays all kinds of surrealistic games with the reader, particularly in jumping in and out of the fictions being created by both authors. Often,

PICTURES OF FIDELMAN and THE TENANTS

the reader will follow along in an event in Lesser's life, only to learn that the event is in Lesser's fiction. The reader is irritated, but he knows how Lesser feels: the boundaries of art and life are not so easily determined.

Malamud is particularly interesting on the notion of the unfinished masterpiece as the only existence that the artist has. Lesser feels he has only one masterpiece in him, and at the moment he finishes *The Promised End*, he will cease to be an artist. He may remain a writer and go on to other things, but never again will he feel the exhilaration of the masters. It is for this reason most of all that he cannot finish his novel. When it is finished he will no longer be a novelist: you cannot tell the dancer from the dance or the novelist from the novel.

CHAPTER SEVEN

DUBIN'S LIVES

T|hough *Dubin's Lives* (1979) follows its hero through two full years of clearly demarcated seasons, the tone of the novel is autumnal. Dubin, as a biographer, is a man who examines minutely the lives of others. At the age of fifty-six, Dubin finds himself looking into the many mirrors in the novel to determine whether he has ever "lived." In his biographies, he has relived the lives of a number of other men, yet he wonders if devotion to his "lives" has been at the cost of his own life. As he approaches old age, he feels he has lived whatever life he will live and wonders if this can be enough?

Though he has the whole countryside at his disposal, Dubin jogs or walks over the same two routes, one short, one long. His life has become nothing more than two such paths: a short one of daily routine and a longer one marked by the seeing through of a biography from inception to publication. In the Vermont landscape, which boasts Robert Frost's farmhouse, Dubin reexamines the premise of Frost's "The Road Not Taken." In the poem, Frost congratulates himself for taking the less well-worn path in his life, but the burden of the poem

DUBIN'S LIVES

lies in the fact that the choices made in life become irrevocable as they lead to further and further choices. That is, each of us has only one life, though an alternative path may have opened for us at some point. In one of the meanings of the novel's title, Dubin questions the singular character of our lives. Dubin, basing his thought on an essay by Montaigne, "That Men Are Not to Judge of Our Happiness Till after Death," discovers that lives can change their character after the fact, that is, the value and meaning of the past can be redetermined by the present. In effect, one can change the path already taken. Life also opens alternatives and possibilities that can change the future as well as the past. Since certain moral choices affect the meaning of both the future and the past, one *can* take "the road not taken."

Dubin is a moral man before he realizes that life will force him to make moral choices. He works hard to define himself and his life. He struggles, using diet and exercise, to fend off the demons of advancing age, and defines himself intellectually through the books he has written, and especially the book he is writing. He has already completed book-length studies of Lincoln, Twain, and Thoreau. Since Dubin is a free-lance biographer with no university connection (Dubin angrily rejects an academic title bestowed on him by an unctuous bellhop), he has no external measure of accomplishment except the work he has done and will do. For this reason, Dubin's work is more than just a living. A university professor is still a professor even when he is not publishing, but when a biographer is not creating a life, he is merely someone who once had an occupation.

UNDERSTANDING BERNARD MALAMUD

When the novel opens, Dubin has undertaken a biography of D. H. Lawrence: a man who wrote that passion was life, but who lived a life that did not match his work—a life, in fact, marked by impotence at an early age. Dubin is something of a romantic, but has never known passion and finds Lawrence to be an uncongenial subject. Dubin struggles to get Lawrence under control, but it may be that Lawrence will defeat him instead. For much of the last half of the novel, Dubin finds himself impotent with his wife.

Dubin's impotence is just one of numerous losses age brings without compensating gains. Dubin sees himself "diminishing," that is, losing the powers and abilities of his manhood. He loses his memory, his sexual powers, his ability to work, even his ability to relate to his family. At first, the only compensation for these losses is a kind of high-grade nostalgia brought about by a process called reverie (Malamud usually uses this noun as a verb). Dubin "reveries" his past to investigate the reasons for and nature of his marriage, his relation to his natural child and his stepchild, the influence of his parents, and the values that he now gives to life. As he examines the past, he discovers that he still has choices to make about the future.

The most important choice that Dubin will make is between his wife, Kitty, and a much younger woman, his part-time housekeeper, Fanny Bick. At first, the two women seem to represent a pair of polar principles. Kitty, who is always smelling for leaking gas, sees life as fear of death, while Fanny, who always has a half-eaten fruit on the seat of her car, ap-

DUBIN'S LIVES

pears to be life-giving and fruitful. Fanny appears for the first time following the description of a flight of birds (always a positive sign in Malamud), and even her orange Volkswagen is citrus-colored. Among the fruits to be found in her car is a half-eaten peach, an allusion to T. S. Eliot's aging J. Alfred Prufrock who wonders if he dare eat a peach, that is, if he dare encounter the opposite sex. When he sends Fanny away even after she has thrown him her lemon-colored underpants, Dubin also appears afraid to take the kind of chance that Prufrock would fear and Lawrence would approve.

Dubin cannot for long ignore Fanny's primary attraction, her exuberant youth that will allow age briefly to forget itself in her arms. He takes Fanny on a trip to Venice where everything goes wrong. Beset by comic confusions that prevent the consummation of the affair, Dubin, in red plaid trousers, becomes a modern version of Pantalone, the cuckolded old husband in the *commedia del arte*, who cannot keep his young wife safe from handsome young men. Dubin is also like two other Renaissance inhabitants of Venice, Othello and Brabantio (whom he quotes). Dubin plays the older husband to a young "wife" and, like Othello, fears that his "young affects are defunct," that is, his sexual power and passion have disappeared. Like Shakespeare's hero, Dubin cannot quite understand how he got the love of such a beautiful young woman.

Dubin is put in the position of Desdemona's father, Brabantio, when he sees someone he thinks is his daughter with a much older black man. The dual roles of father and jealous lover come into conflict and destroy his chance for a romantic fling along the canals. Dubin pursues a woman he thinks is his daughter, Maud, making him late for his assignation with the impatient Fanny, whom he finds making love to that romantic cliché, a singing gondolier. Though the pursuit of his daughter seems an empty chase, it turns out that the girl may have been Maud, who has a black lover Dubin's age and was in Venice at this time. Malamud leaves the mystery intact and will not tell us if Dubin ruined his tryst with Fanny over nothing.

The Venetian catastrophe does not make Dubin a sadder, but wiser man. Instead, he finds that Fanny is becoming an even bigger part of his life. He spends a bleak winter trying to convince himself that he doesn't care about her and refuses to answer her apologetic letters. After a winter of discipline and rigor, Dubin decides, in the spring, to be kind to his life by demanding less out of it and hoping to enjoy it more. After eating an orange (the color of Fanny's Volkswagen), he sets out on a leisurely walk and finds Fanny, now in a white Volvo, eating a peach. This time Dubin dares to eat a peach, and he makes love to Fanny in a field of wild flowers. Malamud uses the wild flowers to set up a subtle symbolism concerning the two women in Dubin's life.

Flowers are positive symbols in Malamud, and Dubin sees this love-making in a field of flowers as a triumph over the wintry aspects of his life. As the flowers are insisted upon and described at great length, the reader is reminded that Kitty's place is also among flowers. She is often seen in her garden, and Fanny first attempts to seduce Dubin when Kitty is off at the nursery buying flowers. The contrast, then, is not between

flowers and no flowers, but between wild flowers and culti-
vated ones. Since both are worthwhile, the flower imagery
suggests the possibility of two valid kinds of love. Furthermore, Dubin dwells on a wild flower called mock orange that
smells like oranges, but will bear no fruit. The reader is to re-
member that real orange blossoms presage the true fruitfulness of marriage.

Even as Dubin becomes comfortable with this duality, it
becomes more complex. Fanny is not nearly so spontaneous
as their idyll among the mock orange suggests. Because she
had read his biography of Mark Twain and was hoping to
benefit from his philosopher's wisdom, she had come to Vermont originally with the intention of meeting Dubin. Several
conclusions are to be drawn from this revelation. First, her being drawn to Dubin through his writing exactly parallels the
way Dubin was attracted by words to Kitty. Second, the fact
of Fanny's premeditation completely recasts all the first mo-
ments of their involvement. What he thought were casual
glances and chance meetings were all manipulated by Fanny.
Such knowledge carries both losses and compensations for
Dubin, who discovers that Fanny's interest in him was less
spontaneous and presumably less passionate than he first be-
lieved, even as he realizes that Fanny is a person of greater
depth (intellectual as well as emotional) than he had sup-
posed. Fanny's revelation also shows how the meaning of the
past can be changed by events in the present.

The affair blossoms into one of full-scale passion as Dubin
begins to meet clandestinely with Fanny in her apartment in

New York (called several times the Big Apple). During the sex act, Fanny offers Dubin a rose with the thorns cut off, apparently symbolizing the ease of passion. This passion—and it is not yet love—improves Dubin's ability to write about D. H. Lawrence, but the guilt it raises makes him impotent in his marriage.

The last stage of the affair occurs when Fanny moves to Center Campobello at about the same time that Kitty is willing to give Dubin a divorce. Fanny buys the neighboring farm and starts breeding goats. For Dubin, this means that a new road has opened in his life. He finds that he loves Fanny, not merely lusts after her. Furthermore, by making love to Fanny on her goat farm, he could out-Lawrence Lawrence, who, in *Women in Love*, can write about sexual encounters in front of domestic animals, but could not personally perform such acts. Dubin can have it all. If he can give up his wife, circumstances will allow him to marry Fanny, or at least live with her openly. At this time, Dubin is living in his barn-study, putting him spatially as well as emotionally equidistant from the two women. He must choose between them.

Dubin's other choice is his wife Kitty. Dubin has to weigh the present with Fanny against the lifetime he has spent with Kitty. The great strike against Kitty, both past and present, is the absence of Lawrentian passion. Dubin's marriage was an American version of the European arranged marriage. Kitty, a widow with a small child, had submitted an object-matrimony letter to the personals section of a newspaper where Dubin worked. Though she had had second thoughts and requested that the ad not be run, Dubin pursued the relationship and eventually they married. This response is typical of Dubin: he responded to the description of her life before he laid eyes on her.

Kitty fulfilled important needs in Dubin's life. He had just determined that he was going to move from writing obituaries to writing biographies. This change from recording the deeds of the dead to bringing the dead to life through his writing required Dubin to revive his own life. Kitty provided the stability and order that his life needed and allowed him to fill the roles that a man takes as part of life: father, husband, and lover. What the marriage lacked was romance on both sides. Dubin, who had been a romantic in his youth (he marries in his early thirties), sees this marriage as a wise thing to do. Kitty had directed her romantic feelings to her first husband, a man whose early death (cancer at forty) helped gloss over his many inadequacies. Even though Kitty loves Dubin, the shadow of her first marriage hangs over her second after twenty years.

Dubin learns from Kitty the art of compromise—yielding part of oneself to another personality—that is marriage. This compromise includes small, but nagging, irritations like a partner's inability to sleep becoming one's own inability to sleep. Sometimes larger issues need to be compromised, as when Dubin and Kitty begin to learn each other's sense of mortality. While Dubin sees death as a force which gradually encroaches through time on life, Kitty sees death as a sudden stalker that takes life in a moment, the way it took her husband. For this reason, she is always fearful of death the killer and cannot leave the house without smelling the burners for gas. Dubin is sensitive to his wife's obsession and hides the fact that he has run over the cat. It is not surprising that Dubin's first work, written partly under Kitty's sway, was a collection of short biographies of men who lived short lives. The collection is called appropriately *Short Lives*.

Despite the tension in the marriage, it has generally been a good one, with positive values added on both sides. Dubin has proved to be a good father to Kitty's son Gerald as well as to their mutual daughter, Maud. During the present time of the novel, the lives of both now-adult children fall apart, giving Dubin reason to question the value of marriage in its function of producing and raising children.

Dubin's trouble with the marriage comes partly from his relations with Fanny, but largely from a growing sense of his own isolation from the rest of the human community, including his wife. As a biographer of Thoreau, Dubin treasures solitude, but often finds it difficult to distinguish solitude from loneliness. In the course of the novel, Dubin breaks off relations with his best friend, moves his study from the house to the barn, and alienates himself from both his adopted son and his natural daughter. In each case, Dubin finally moves toward a partial restoration of human relationships.

Dubin insists so obsessively on solitude because he fears wasting time. Only his work and his regimen matter in his determination of what wasted time is. He begrudges hours lost when he cannot sleep, hours lost thinking about Fanny, hours lost worrying about domestic trifles. Dubin is appalled at two

DUBIN'S LIVES

great examples of wasting time: his son's life lived as a deserter from the army and his daughter's dilettantism and her affair with an older man. Dubin consoles himself with Thoreau's insight that all great work is created at the expense of a life, until his daughter, a notorious waster of time, reminds him that almost all living is a "waste" of time.

Dubin sees life as a vocation fulfilled by making choices. For this reason, he chooses to become a biographer at the same time he chooses to marry. Both decisions end a drifting period in his life—one occupational, the other personal. In a lovely chapter, Malamud counterpoints a reverie of Dubin's early marriage against his meeting with his son Gerald. At first the situations of father and son seem similar. Dubin chose marriage, it did not happen to him, just as Gerald chose desertion with three months to serve. The difference is that Dubin continues to choose, while for Gerald life has become barren of alternatives. When a man stops making choices, he no longer lives life, it lives him. Gerald gives up all his earlier industry—his study of biology with the possibility of becoming a doctor and his study of Swedish. Eventually he will drift into greater trouble in Russia. Though such a slide might be considered life, it is a waste of time.

The situation of Dubin's daughter is somewhat different, though it seems she will end up about as bad off as Gerald. Maud *is* a chooser; she makes choices all the time, but these choices seem no more than the expression of dilettantism. One can choose too much, and one can choose too little. When we see Maud go off to a Zen commune we can only expect the worst, and in a sense, the worst happens. She gets pregnant by a man she has tried to leave behind. He turns out to be her Spanish instructor, who is married, black, and Dubin's age. Dubin, with Fanny on his conscience is hard-pressed to criticize his daughter, but he learns something in listening to her. She has chosen her life. She has chosen to love a man she ought not to love, but whatever her error, it is her choice and it is her life. The rightness of her choice is hinted at in a footnote to the novel which tells us that she collaborated with Dubin on his last biography (of Anna Freud) and that she apparently married her lover. The fact that Dubin turns to the daughter of a genius for his last work, suggests that he has returned fully to his relationship with his daughter.

Though Dubin always thinks about life and lives, he has not been so honest with death. Dubin's assumptions about death and life are revised in two shocking confrontations with primal forces. The two events, a blizzard in the woods and an attack by a dog on a farm, are neatly paralleled at the end of chapters one third and two-thirds of the way through the novel. The first of these events, the blizzard, occurs at the end of the chapter that recounts his reaction to his unsuccessful trip to Venice with Fanny. Dubin finds that the small lies he has told to maintain the secrecy of the botched affair have begun to eat away at him both physically and emotionally. To combat the diminishing—the gain of weight, the inability to write, the inability to talk to his wife—he sets himself a regimen in which he will take on the spirit of winter itself. He gets up at dawn each day to walk five miles in the Vermont winter. He believes that self-discipline alone will be enough to reshape his life. This belief is shattered when Dubin finds himself lost in a blizzard. Dubin wanders in circles through a landscape out of Robert Frost's poetry. When he loses the road in the blinding storm, he realizes how little—only a step—it takes to get off the right path into the uncharted wilderness of life. Dubin feels that his straying with Fanny has led him to a blizzard of unleashed emotions, though the blizzard he is walking through is real not metaphorical. His wandering brings him across the path of an auto in which his wife is waiting for him. If this were the end of the novel, the implication would be clear: stay on the straight and narrow path and your life will be secure.

That things are not so clear is suggested by two bird symbols that frame the blizzard episode. The first is in the mystic mood of *The Magic Barrel*. Dubin meets a stranger on the road and in his pedantic way points out Frost's farmhouse. The man mimes shooting down a blackbird with a nonexistent gun. Though the gun is imaginary, the blackbird, to the man's shout of "bang bang," falls unwounded into the snow. Dubin can only speculate on the possibility of blackbirds having heart attacks. What seems to have happened is that the poetic world of Frost has leaked into reality. Though blackbirds may not have heart attacks, in heart ailments Malamud often signifies failures of love. The death of the blackbird is a warning to the middle-aged Dubin that to be out of tune with the season like the blackbird in the white field is to expose oneself to mysterious and deadly forces.

The bird at the other side of the frame is a white owl. While lost in the blizzard, Dubin has to decide whether to stay in the woods or go back to the unmarked fields. He cannot make up his mind until a white owl showers snow on him and then flees the wood. Dubin follows the owl's example and takes to the open himself—a decision which saves his life. When Dubin finds his wife waiting for him, he has only one sentence to say, "I saw a white owl." The protective coloration of the owl suggests that Dubin must put himself back in harmony with nature rather than struggling against it as he had in his quasi-military treks through the snow. In the following chapter, Dubin ceases his struggle against winter, he stops crossing off its days and waiting for spring. Winter is life, too.

Dubin is more successful in coming to terms with nature than in coming to terms with other human beings, and a second confrontation in the woods ends a chapter in which Dubin wounds almost all of his friends. He has offended one friend, a psychiatrist, by suggesting that his method of healing is a fraud, he turns Kitty against him by naming Fanny as his lover, and he is confronted by his best friend, Greenfeld, who had had a heart attack in Europe while Dubin was sleeping with his wife in Vermont (as with the blackbird, the connection of the adultery and the heart attack is symbolic not medical). In each case, Dubin trespasses on the rights of others.

Dubin finds himself fleeing from all these collapsing friendships and from his inability to write his book. Instead of the birdshooting stranger, Dubin is haunted by the ghost of Lady Chatterley's lover who is accusing him of being afraid to live life to its fullest. No longer in shape, Dubin flees in a car this time and soon finds himself literally and figuratively out of gas on a country road. He wanders into a farm family's grave-yard where he finds the names on the stones worn away by time and the weather: a clear warning to the biographer that he must make his mark indelibly, or his life, too, will end up unnoted. He then falls into an open grave, reminding him that we all live on the edge of the pit. Before he can get to the farm-er's house to telephone for help, he is attacked by the farmer's dog. The farmer comes out to shoot the trespasser but shoots his own dog instead. Dubin sees this as no chance event but as a logical and symbolic concatenation of events that led him out of his own house to a place where he has caused a man to kill his own dog. Nothing in life is without meaning, and if you trespass on another man's land or flee your responsibil-ities, dire results are inevitable. Dubin escapes from the wood and this time finds Fanny waiting for him.

This time there are no reservations in the love affair. Fanny proves to be a woman of far greater maturity than Dubin had imagined, and her plans to become a lawyer no longer seem far-fetched. As Dubin helps Fanny arrange her legal edu-cation, the Lawrentian fantasy of love among the livestock, to no one's disappointment, fades. Dubin finds he no longer has the egotistical need to live more fully than the subjects of his biographies. He also learns something else as he helps prepare Fanny for a career that will not start for at least four years— her life is ahead of her, but his is not. This is not a matter of age, but experience. He has lived a full life, and it is a life he has shared with Kitty. He has lived enough of a life to make himself the subject of a biography (the one that Malamud has written for him), while Fanny has not. Again this is not a matter of age, Dubin has written lives of people who died younger than Fanny is now. Because she has not yet examined her life, Fanny cannot understand what Dubin means when he tells her that he loves her, but loves Kitty's life. For the biographer the choice is simple, and he takes the passion and romance that he has learned from Fanny and brings it home to the woman who has shared his life. The suggestion is that this gift will be at least half-appreciated.

CHAPTER EIGHT

GOD'S GRACE

T|his fable about life after the atomic holocaust is built on the structure of a number of parallel stories, most of which are biblical or Shakespearean (the books owned by the hero include *The Works of Shakespeare*, a Pentateuch, a dictionary, and Walther Bünder's *The Great Apes*). Among the most important analogs are the stories of Romeo and Juliet, Abraham and Isaac, and Jacob and Esau. As is typical in Malamud's retellings of old myths (the Grail legend in *The Natural*, the St. Francis story in *The Assistant*), the point of the new version is to examine and often change the values presented in the old. In this novel, most of the analogs are more explicitly presented than in Malamud's other work. The characters tell each other the stories or are given names which make their literary antecedents quite obvious. Perhaps this is because Malamud takes such liberties in reshaping the original tales that he wants the parallels clearly seen. In *God's Grace*, the Isaac figure sacrifices Abraham, and no ram appears to take the victim's place, the Romeo of the piece falls in love with a Juliet who is a chimpanzee, and it is Esau rather than Jacob who gets his father's birthright.

One of the most important analogs is a Shakespearean play that is not explicitly named in the text. In *The Tempest*, Prospero, an overeducated duke, lands on a tiny island and usurps the throne of Caliban, the island's beastlike king and only inhabitant. Prospero then imposes his theoretically perfect laws on the island, hoping to turn the savage Caliban into a civilized man. By the time the play starts, Prospero's experiment with Caliban has already failed, but it takes Prospero the length of the play to realize that his bookish scheme has entirely excluded the beast's point of view. In *God's Grace*, the Prospero figure is a paleontologist named Calvin Cohn who was undersea when mankind destroyed itself by nuclear holocaust, followed by universal flood.

Cohn, the last man on earth (God, in a conversation with Cohn, admits that his survival is a tiny error), finds himself on an island with several chimps, including one who can talk, and a gorilla who likes to listen to Hebrew chants recorded by Cohn's father. Cohn sets out to civilize the chimps and to build a little nation on the island. Like Prospero, he never really accepts the intelligence of the other beings there. Forgetting or ignoring that it was civilized man who destroyed the world, Cohn tries to mold the apes into his image.

Cohn begins in Robinson Crusoe fashion with a chimp who has been given the power of speech through an artificial larynx implanted by the late Dr. Walther Bünder, another scientist from Cohn's research ship. Much of the interest of

GOD'S GRACE

the first part of the book lies in watching Cohn and his "man Friday" reestablish the material elements of civilization out of the wreckage of the ship and the natural products of the island. A father-son relationship develops between man and chimp, with the chimp calling Cohn "Dod" (the chimp never completely gets rid of the German accent Bünder taught him). Cohn seems jealous of Bünder's original fatherly role toward the chimp, and changes the chimp's name from Gottlob to Buz.

Like many of Malamud's heroes, Cohn is a lapsed Jew. He had changed his first name from the "Seymour" his father gave him to Calvin, perhaps more than coincidentally the name of the Protestant reformer. Cohn had also given up his rabbinic studies to become a paleontologist because he was always interested in the beginnings of things. His Judaism had slipped to little more than an interest in God as First Cause, but on his island, Cohn wants to make better Jews of the chimps than he is himself. This attempt to improve others always comes out, Prospero-like, better in theory than practice. Despite Cohn's humble demeanor, he is exceedingly proud of his species, his religion, his culture, and his wisdom (in this he is like another island-dweller, Gulliver). Cohn sets himself up as supreme lawgiver with a set of principles based, like Prospero's, on reason rather than holiness or love. Though he acts diffident about his wisdom, he never defers to the judgment of anyone else. A student of beginnings, Cohn doesn't realize that he is ill-equipped to comprehend the end of things.

For Cohn, man's wisdom begins with his command of language. Speech is the supreme gift of mankind: the source not merely of culture, but of civilization itself. He tells Buz that language alone makes man superior to the apes. Cohn sidesteps Buz's accurate response that man's superiority of language has brought him within one *man* of annihilation. Cohn's view of language is entirely anthropocentric. He hopes for the apes to learn man's language; it never occurs to him to learn theirs. Though he has a copy of Shakespeare, Cohn has never considered Caliban's complaint, "You taught me language; and my profit on't is, I know how to curse." What neither Prospero nor Cohn have learned is that communication is a sharing of ideas rather than the dominance of one set of ideas over another.

This begins with the naming of names. In *The Tempest*, Caliban reminds us that naming process had gone only one way: "Thou . . . wouldst . . . teach me how to name the bigger light, and how the less." As with Cohn and the apes, it had never occurred to Prospero to ask Caliban what he called the sun and the moon, or even the plants indigenous to the island; it was Caliban's island after all. Cohn likewise tries to reserve to himself the right of naming. Though he considers naming the island "Chimpan Zee" after the more populous species, he opts for the self-flattering "Cohn's Island." He plants a sign with this name on it, and though he notes the pride involved in giving the island this name, he never gets around to taking down the sign. Cohn, in fact, is full of good intentions that never materialize into actions.

Not only does he rename Buz, he also takes offense when Buz names the first group of new chimpanzees (largely after

GOD'S GRACE

New Testament figures—Mary Madelyn, Luke, Saul of Tarsus). Cohn petulantly claims Adam's right of naming for himself, somehow forgetting that he is the last man instead of the first. As always when he is called on in such matters, Cohn expresses liberal and rather paternalistic sentiments: Buz can name things as long as he checks with Cohn first. When another opportunity presents itself, however, Cohn rushes to name a second group of new chimps before Buz can have any say in the matter. He names them after an insignificant aunt of his and two nearly forgotten college friends. Compared to the biblical names chosen by Buz, Cohn's names seem trivial and his rush to name the chimps, petty.

Cohn sets himself up as teacher, really guru, for the island, yet the greatest task of teaching is successfully undertaken by Buz. Though he has been taught to speak through the use of an artificial larynx, Buz is able to teach the other chimps to speak without any man-made device. At a time when Cohn's educational goals for the apes were a few sign language gestures a day, Buz teaches them enough English to read and care about Shakespeare. Instead of seeing this as a sign of the chimp's superiority (Buz is only a boy, having recently reached puberty), Cohn almost ignores his accomplishment and goes on to use Buz's work to teach the apes his versions of history and morality.

Buz, at this point, offers Cohn two important lessons. First, his teaching the apes to speak is an act of faith, that is, as long as they believe in Buz, believe in themselves, and believe in each other, they can communicate in any language, even

Cohn's English. Since Cohn does not believe in them as intelligent beings, he never learns to communicate with them in their language. At the close of the novel this will prove to be a fatal flaw. Second, Buz reminds Cohn that the chimps do not need the human race to know what is going on in the world. Cohn, the teacher, is a poor student. He never pays any attention to the ape point of view, and his faith is never anything more than a lukewarm trust in benevolent rationalism.

After asserting that language is the peculiarly human institution, Cohn takes little note when the hard-working Buz masters the language to the point where he is able to correct Cohn's grammar. He doesn't see that Buz's superiority in usage and grammar marks a superiority in morality as well. Buz points out the inconsistency in Cohn's attitudes. He hears the hollow ring when Cohn says he doesn't want personal power but only wants to be the chimps' "protector." He knows that Cohn's offering "a certain amount of reasonable direction" means things will be done Cohn's way.

Compared to Buz, Cohn is always petty in his conceptions. He wonders, based on simian "bathroom" habits, whether gorillas or chimps are more civilized, yet he never sees that atomic bomb-wielding men are less civilized than coconut-wielding gorillas. Cohn even fails to appreciate the symbolic use of language. Cohn is far too literal when he sees Buz eat pages of books or the gorilla, George, eat a phonograph record. All Cohn can see is paper and recording wax as odd ape delicacies, when the eating of words actually symbolizes the apes' desire to devour the knowledge that Cohn touts so highly. Nor does he realize that a mysterious white ape is his alter ego on the island. Cohn had been successful using witch's masks to frighten off the apes when they threatened him. The white ape, however, tears the mask from Cohn and puts it over his own face. Cohn misses the point: man is nothing more than a white primate with a human face. Had he learned that much, he would never have treated the other apes as his inferiors. Later, Cohn mistaking the white ape for an enemy chimp, kills him, thus violating his own first admonition, "Thou shalt not kill." One can only surmise that God as he watches Cohn becoming a Cain to the white ape's Abel, finally shuts the door on the possible survival of the human race.

Cohn's teachings under the learning tree are attempts to humanize the apes, always assuming that the human way is best, even though he tells himself that what he wants is for "them to understand themselves and fulfill the social contract." His nonspecies-oriented word is "civilize," which for Cohn means "humanize." In the context of nuclear devastation, this calls for a good deal of rationalizing about human behavior. Cohn's explanation of the holocaust uses a tricky leap from Freud to make mankind's self-destruction bestial rather than rational. He argues that man destroyed himself because he did not use reason (ego) to control his animal nature (id). Freud in fact says that war is an expression of repressed instinctual behavior, both sexual and aggressive. This repression is necessary for there to be work, which is the foundation of civilization. Cohn builds his society on the premise that it is good to civilize those who need civilizing, yet he never considers the other side of Freud's theory, which points out that all civilization is hypocrisy since humans are continually repressing their natural (not bestial) desires. Even though the first purpose of his society is the distribution of fruit, Cohn never questions the need for work on an island that seems to have enough fruit for everyone. Likewise he does not question the need for sexual morality, even though the chimps' sexual behavior would normally be controlled by the seasons and natural cycles. Most of the chimps, including Buz, accept Cohn's statement of the reality principle (instincts must be suppressed so that work can be done). Only Esau, the most vicious (and to Cohn the most bestial) of the chimps, challenges the need to work or to deny sexual and aggressive instincts. Since Cohn has already written off Esau as renegade and troublemaker, he pays no attention to him.

In addition to Freud, the genius of Einstein haunts the novel. The physicist's pure application of intellect conceived that E equaled MC^2 and gave the world atomic power (in his sublimating phase, Buz directs his sexual frustration toward algebra. Can nuclear physics be far behind?). At his school-tree, Cohn wants the apes to become civilized and learn the lessons of both Freud and Einstein. Both modern giants, both Jews, were looking for total control of nature, one human, the other physical. Such control is civilization; Cohn never questions its value.

Though he is a lapsed Jew, Cohn tries to impose Judaism upon the apes, but it is a Judaism gutted of its heart. Cohn's religion takes the form of negation, so that when Buz tries to put his fingers on a picture of Jessica (Shylock's daughter in *The Merchant of Venice*), Cohn pushes him away more because he sees him as a gentile than as a nonhuman. Though he calls Buz both son and brother, he doesn't want him fooling with any of the daughters of Abraham.

Cohn holds a Passover service for the apes, with tropical versions of the necessary ingredients (baked eggs, bitter herbs, shankbone of lamb, etc.). In the process he reduces the seder to a secular event. The Four Questions, which traditionally begin the explanation of the Passover, become a questionnaire into the personal history of the apes. Like most of Malamud's heroes, most notably Bok in *The Fixer*, Cohn keeps up a one-sided ironic dialog with God as he questions the suffering of the Jews and of mankind. The difference between Bok and Cohn is that Bok is a genuine agnostic looking for the truth, while Cohn plays the game because he has nothing else to do. Though he tells Buz there will be freedom of religion on his island, he refuses to accept the possibility of any other religion but his own, even though he no longer believes in it.

Instead of the Ten Commandments, Cohn creates his own rules which he calls the Seven Admonitions (Cohn refuses to think of himself as an autocrat). Though he thinks of his admonitions as nonbiased, they constitute a slightly softer-voiced Judaism than the Ten Commandments. The key admonition, and a direct denial of Christianity, is "God is not love, God is God." When Buz, who by the end of the novel becomes a Christlike preacher to the multitudes (all nine of the apes), scratches out the "not," Cohn is furious with the chimp's *chutzpah*. Only Cohn gets to make the religion on Cohn's Island. Rather than argue with the apes, however, he is ready to scratch the whole admonition, but he is too late. Mary Madelyn has learned to announce "God is love" with a breathy space where the "not" has been scratched out. Unable to make sense of the universe as God has given it, Cohn is unwilling to admit that any other notion of God exists.

Cohn's plans to civilize the apes through his Seven Admonitions make him into a Mosaic lawgiver (he puts an image of Moses on the wine goblet he makes for himself). Besides being a lawgiver, he is like Moses in a more tragic way. Moses, because he questioned the commandment of God and struck a rock instead of speaking to it, was condemned never to enter the promised land. Like Moses, Cohn may lead the way to a new world, but neither he nor his seed will enter it.

When Cohn questions God's wisdom in creating imperfect man to complete his perfect idea of the world, God answers his presumption by appearing in a pillar of fire and then raining lemons on his head. Cohn is speechless. Never really adaptable, he doesn't learn what the apes figure out: if God gives you lemons, make lemonade.

In contrast to Cohn's failing faith, Buz holds staunchly to his Christianity. Buz offers Cohn a crucifix which Cohn takes only to get it away from Buz. He refuses to wear it himself, and when Buz is ready to get it back, his neck has grown too large for the chain. Cohn does not suspect that the crucifix will mark him as the sacrificial victim and that he may be the

GOD'S GRACE

Christ of the new society rather than its Moses or its Abraham. The hubristic presumption that he is the Abraham of the new order occurs when Cohn takes the female chimpanzee, Mary Madelyn, as his "bride." Here Cohn's anti-simian prejudice shows through, since the articulate chimp Buz is the ideal choice to be her mate. There is no reason why Buz's genes would not produce an entirely acceptable creature, except that it would not resemble human beings in face and figure. Though he is a paleontologist who has spent his life recording the infinitesimal changes that produce new species, Cohn thinks he can speed up evolution by plugging his genes directly into the cosmic scheme, saving eons with one bang (a novel version of the big-bang theory of the beginnings of the universe). Cohn's change of first name from Seymour to Calvin permits another outrageous pun as well. Instead of Calvin Klein, maker of designer jeans, Malamud gives us Calvin Cohn, creator of designer genes. Cohn sees himself as the father of a new species, half-man, half-chimp: a new race dominant over the earth sprung from his seed. To do this would be to go Abraham one better, since he was only father of the Jews.

As in almost all of his rationalizations, Cohn wants things both ways. When Buz complains that Mary Madelyn will not present herself to him chimp-style, Cohn suggests that Mary Madelyn would rather be courted than mounted. Then having taught her romantic love out of *Romeo and Juliet*, he himself woos her in ways Buz cannot. Nowhere is Cohn so pompous as when he tells the frustrated Buz to sublimate his lust. Buz spends his time polishing stones and doing algebra, and one suspects that if he had kept on he would have reinvented money and nuclear physics. Cohn tells the other young male chimp, Esau, to masturbate, and his frustration leads to the violence that destroys Cohn's civilization.

Cohn has to rationalize on a grand scale to justify his mating with Mary Madelyn. He has to deal first of all with a Talmudic prohibition against intercourse with animals that requires both the death of the man and of the beast he defiles. He argues to himself that Mary Madelyn is an intelligent creature and therefore no beast. But if she is no beast then neither is Buz, and Cohn still has no business mating with her. Cohn will never admit that his motivations are as basic as Buz's: he is horny. In fact, unless he mates with Mary Madelyn, he will be horny forever because there are no more human women.

Even when he mates with another species, Cohn maintains his racial-religious bias. He insists that the child conceived from the union have a Jewish name and even urges Mary Madelyn to change her name to Rachel so that he will feel more comfortable with her. Talk about *chutzpah*! When Mary Madelyn suggests they, like Romeo and Juliet, marry, Cohn says he will consider a wedding if it is Jewish . . . for his father's sake. As with his good intentions about removing the sign that proclaims Cohn's Island, Cohn fails here, too. He never gets around to marrying Mary Madelyn.

Though he is continually humane with the other chimps on the island, Cohn is never really human. He may put a dress on Mary Madelyn, he may teach her *Romeo and Juliet* (though he holds out, unfairly, on its tragic end), but he never thinks of her as another equal being. For this reason, he always equivocates when she asks if he loves her. She firmly avows her love for him, but he always replies with "I think so" or "sure." When he cites the biblical injunction against lying with cattle, she asserts that she is not cattle and rightly asks Cohn if he has a mind of his own.

Cohn is also humane with Esau, the ferocious chimp who, with Buz, is his rival for Mary Madelyn. Cohn temporarily wins Esau's service and acquiescence to the work ethic by removing an infected tooth. This is no story of Androcles and the lion, and Esau soon returns to his fierce ways. What Cohn will not accept is that Esau's aggressiveness is natural and, therefore, a part of God's plan. He sees Esau's savage attack on a baboon as inhuman and banishes him. When Esau kills Cohn's half-chimp daughter, Cohn vengefully pursues him with his spear and mistakenly kills the white ape instead of Esau. In this act, Cohn becomes a murderer, no better than the chimp he had condemned.

Central to the novel is Cohn's relationship to the chimp Gottlob, whom Cohn renames Buz despite the chimp's passive objections. Cohn renames Buz in the hope of turning the chimp into a nice Jewish boy, even though Cohn finds him with a crucifix around his neck. Cohn dislikes the name given to the chimp by Bünder because its translation, "praise God," sounds Christian and because its German origins remind him of the Nazi Holocaust. Cohn chooses a most insignificant Old Testament name (Buz was one of many sons of Abraham's brother, Nahor), suggesting that his attempt to convert the chimp is trivial or petty. Cohn knows that it is against Jewish doctrine to proselytize, but his handling of the apes has the quality of missionary work.

Buz accepts Cohn as a father figure and advances far more quickly in language and learning than any father has a right to expect. Nonetheless, Cohn never sees his foster son's progress as anything more than rudimentary. He is as insensitive to the boy's ideas as Prospero is to those of his daughter, Miranda. When Miranda properly counsels her father to be less harsh with a stranger, the outraged Prospero demands, "What! My foot, my tutor!" Though Cohn is less forbidding in tone, he would no more accept wisdom from Buz than a head would take instructions from a foot. Throughout the novel, Buz complains that his (and the apes') ideas are never taken seriously by Cohn. Cohn continues to mouth liberal platitudes, but he never believes in them. Despite his memories of Hitler and that Holocaust, Cohn never doubts for a moment that he is the last surviving member of the master race.

Of all the stories that Cohn tells his boy, Buz's favorite is that of Abraham and Isaac. Though Cohn begins with the simple explanation that the would-be sacrifice was a test of Abraham's love for God, he and Buz go on to discuss more complex explanations, including the Freudian one that Abraham wanted to kill his son as a possible rival. Cohn also introduces Kierkegaard's interpretation (in *Fear and Trembling*), though he wrongly equates Kierkegaard's view with Freud's. In fact, Kierkegaard puts the test in terms that Cohn would not understand. Kierkegaard argues that the sacrifice was a true test of faith *because* it was absurd. Cohn's religion, despite its Talmudic leaning on riddles, is ultimately rational and has no place for the absurd.

Cohn's insensitivity is also revealed when he further suggests that the appearance of the ram to take Isaac's place was a sign from God that he wanted to replace the inhumane practice of human sacrifice with animal sacrifice. Not surprisingly, Buz takes no comfort from this solution. For the Christian Buz, the happy ending (Isaac's escape) makes sense only if God is love. Otherwise the more sinister implications, especially the Freudian one, apply. Cohn's Talmudic experience knows no such dogma and in his Seven Admonitions, he specifically denies Buz's claim that "God is love." For Cohn, the Abraham and Isaac story goes only one way. Abraham proves he loves God, not vice versa. Though he will not admit it to his son, this is what has been troubling him from Hitler's Holocaust (Does God love or even care about the Jews?) to the atomic holocaust (Does God love or even care about mankind?). Cohn also reveals that his interest in God is intellectual rather than spiritual. As a scientist, instead of the rabbi he might have been, he wants to know about God rather than know God.

Cohn's concern with Buz's religion stems from his feeling that he has failed his father—by giving up his rabbinical studies, by changing his own name, and by losing his faith. It is too late to change himself, but since the chimp is capable of great faith, he might become a worthy son. This will matter only if Buz becomes a Jew. To this end, he holds the seder, tells Buz Old Testament stories only, and dreams of a bar mitzvah for his boy. All to no avail. Buz refuses to give up his faith, and, in fact, crosses himself during the seder.

Though Buz is willing to follow his dod even against the other apes, their falling-out comes over the female chimp, Mary Madelyn. Cohn takes the female for himself because he is too prejudiced to admit that Buz already possesses all the traits—literacy, intelligence, and moral sense—that Cohn hopes to breed through his own genes. Despite high-sounding justifications, Cohn's taking of the female ape is nothing more than the act of a beast: the strongest male gets the most attractive, and, in this case, the only available, female.

After Cohn mates with Mary Madelyn in the name of civilization, the relationship between Buz and his dod degenerates into a series of ironic exchanges until Buz betrays Cohn by getting him to take down the wall that protects Cohn's half-chimp daughter, Rebekah. When the other chimps kill Rebekah, Cohn retaliates by destroying Buz's artificial larynx. Cohn's act is perhaps the most savage in the book since it denies Buz's humanity and therefore the humanity of all the other chimps. Since all Cohn's moral decisions are based on the humanity of the chimps, he becomes parodoxically bestial and hypocritical in the same act.

The speech of the other chimps was an act of faith in Buz. When he is silenced, they, too, lose the power of speech, as well as many other accomplishments of civilization. Mary Madelyn, despite Cohn's too-late cries of "love, love, love," gives herself ape-fashion to both Buz and his rival Esau, and civilization *as we know it* comes to an end.

All that remains is the working out of the Abraham and Isaac story. In this version, Isaac (Buz) carries his father (Cohn) up the mountainside to be sacrificed. This time no ram appears, and to the Hebrew chanting of George the gorilla, Cohn's throat is cut and the human race comes to an end.

On the face of it, the end makes the title merely ironic— God's grace is no grace at all—but this is to view things as Cohn always had, from a human perspective. Cohn had speculated that God needs man's worship, that man is made in God's image, or even vice versa, but these notions are all anthropocentric. If apes can have ritual, if a gorilla can say Kaddish, who is to say that they are not made in God's image also? Perhaps it is God's grace not to let man contaminate earth any longer. Perhaps it is God's grace to let Cohn live long enough to see that though man no longer exists, God does. This is, after all, the Old Testament name for God—not I am Good, or I am Love, but simply *I Am*. This is the whole of the mystery, and it doesn't matter whether man is there to appreciate it or not.

CHAPTER NINE

SHORT STORIES

T he surprising thing about Malamud's short fiction is that we recognize ourselves in his characters. None of us are like them; we are not that wretched, and we have more style—at least, we have some style. The recognition is not like that felt when we read Philip Roth who seems to have met our uncles and our teachers and our army sergeants and our college roommates and has gotten down their gestures and voices and attitudes perfectly. Nor is the recognition like that felt (at least by intellectuals or those with pretensions toward intellect) when reading Saul Bellow, whose characters, whether quiz show contestants or gangsters, seem to have struggled with every intellectual problem ever faced by thinking man. The ideas are familiar, even if the solutions are new. We don't get that sense of familiarity in Malamud. We've never met his characters before, and yet the shock of recognition is much deeper. They are us. The reader's moment of recognition in reading Malamud is the same as that of the well-dressed banker who looks at one of Rouault's tragic clowns and wonders how the painter could know so much about the banker's inner self; it is like the moment when a well-trained athlete looks at Modigliani's gaunt, skeletal men and sees his true self, weak and frightened, which he has hidden under all his painstakingly built musculature. The characters in Malamud's short fiction are recognizable because they show us ourselves an inch below the skin. What is recognizable is our most essential passions: we are that wretched. We give ourselves over to love or hate or fear so elemental that no external value matters—not the manners limned so accurately by Roth or the ideas traced so complexly by Bellow. Though almost all the characters in the short stories are Jewish, perhaps of the three writers, it is least essential to be Jewish in order to recognize oneself in the characters of Malamud.

In his short stories, Malamud keeps the reader on the cutting edge of emotion through the intensity of his characters, all of whom have occupations, but rarely have functions other than their relations with another person. The characters are seldom seen working at their jobs (though almost all work very hard), and when they are seen working, their work becomes a metaphor for their emotion or sometimes the emotion itself. Malamud's characters will make shoes because of love, press pants out of hate, or paint pictures to combat loneliness or guilt. All of their energies are directed toward their emotions, yet their tales are told in such spare, ironic prose that they rarely become sentimental. Sentimentality is also avoided because opposing kinds of emotional energy are often seen to be twin aspects of the same elemental force. Thus love and hate are almost always conjoined, and charity is never so tender as when it is most ferocious. This is no matter of Freudian sublimation in which the repression of some emotion becomes another, but rather a recognition of the duality of human nature—that the greatest pride is often found in obstinate humility and that the most religious men are usually not those who seek God or the spirit, but those who look to understand themselves or to help their fellow man.

Pascal says man has developed the need for *divertissement* ("diversion") to keep him from the most frightening of all activities: contemplation of his own condition. There is no *divertissement* in Malamud's short fiction. His characters do not play, they do not worry about the latest styles or the newest cars or contemporary politics. Instead they constantly have to face the fearsomeness of their own nature. This lack of diversion does not always lead to pessimism as might be expected. Rather single-mindedness taken to an extreme often uncovers resources the characters never knew they possessed—and the reader shares this knowledge with the characters.

Malamud's characters also take the reader into other realms unexplored by most of his contemporaries. His characters often find the mystical when they least expect it. The world of the spirit is wonderfully accessible in Malamud's short stories because mystic creatures manifest themselves in the most ordinary forms without losing their power to amaze. The Angel of Death *must* look like the hard-hearted Ginzburg in "Idiots First." After we read Malamud we realize we have met this creature before: we have seen that strange gaunt face on the edge of our consciousness. He is no longer a vague concept, but a real being, and his reality is responsible for the way that Malamud's fiction haunts us. The *dybbuks* (evil spirits or the souls of dead men in living bodies), like Susskind in "The Last Mohican," who haunt Malamud's heroes are also typical of how familiar the supernatural is in his fiction. Susskind appears to be an ordinary man, a presumptuous beggar at most, yet he has the power to lead Fidelman in and out of dreams and then out of himself and toward God. And the reader does not say, "How absurd!" but, "Yes! it is possible and besides, I think I once ran into a man like that and if I had only . . ." In reading Malamud, it is not so much a question of suspending one's disbelief, but of doing just the opposite, allowing that belief that has been repressed since the Age of Reason to resurface.

Malamud's spirituality convinces us because he is able to put the mystical in the most mundane settings and then have us believe in both. With a perfect sense of timing, he gradually reveals that two men speaking to each other in "Take Pity" are a dead man and the angel sent to record the dead man's charity. The reader has just begun to wonder what language, older than Hebrew, one of the men is writing, when he realizes with a shiver that the other is about to tell how he took his own life trying to be charitable to a woman. This shiver is nothing to the one felt when the room in which the two are conversing turns out to be the grave, and the dead man looks out a window and sees the woman, still alive, trying to apologize for being too proud to accept the man's charity when he was alive.

Malamud does this again and again. By the time the mystical is upon us, it is just ordinary enough for us to accept it.

Often this is because Malamud's characters accept it first. When a loving father in "Idiots First" races to put his idiot son on the day's last train to California, it slowly dawns on the father that the man trying to stop him is no bill collector or social worker, but the Angel of Death. Once the reader accepts this, he is awed but not surprised when the father bests the angel in a struggle which is literally beyond life and death. The reader is in Grand Central Station and in the realm of the spirit at the same time.

At this point, metaphors resonate into something larger: in "The Loan," burnt loaves in a baker's oven no longer *resemble* the corpses in Hitler's incinerators; they are the corpses in Hitler's incinerators. A "Talking Horse" is not, as the reader first suspects, a man in a horse costume, but a real talking horse. Just when the reader has convinced himself that this makes sense, Malamud turns him again and reveals that the talking horse is really a centaur who has been mysteriously locked into the flesh-and-blood upper half of a horse—a costume, but one unlike any ever seen before. The reader is surprised, but acquiesces; this, too, makes sense. Malamud has worked his magic, and the last wave of the wand reveals that this centaur is in many ways ordinary enough to face the same human problems as the reader.

Malamud can make anyone human. When a Jewish bird helps junior with his homework, it is not surprising because the bird sounds exactly like a helpful "Jewbird." He *kvetches* ("whines"), mooches, spouts homely wisdom, worries about the availability of herring, and fears anti-Semitism from one

SHORT STORIES

of its most dangerous sources—Jews who have forgotten what Judaism means. That the fate of this upstart crow is felt as tragedy is a further tribute to Malamud's genius for merging the miraculous with the ordinary.

The short stories of Malamud (now collected in one volume) originally appeared in three collections, *The Magic Barrel*, *Idiots First*, and *Rembrandt's Hat*. Almost all are tight, spare stories that revolve around the relations of two, sometimes three, characters. The themes are freedom, commitment, responsibility, and the bonds of love and hate that link man to man. Most have Jews as their central characters, though sometimes, these Jews take surprising forms: there is a black guardian angel in "Angel Levine," an intrusive bird in "The Jewbird," and Jewish centaur in "Talking Horse." Though most of the stories take place in urban Jewish settings, there is a large fraction of Malamud's short fiction set in Italy (where he lived in 1956). Even among these, the main characters are often Jewish, and a group of the Italian stories has been regathered into a picaresque novel, *Pictures of Fidelman*.

"Man in a Drawer," the longest of Malamud's short stories, brings together many of the themes that are found in his short fiction. The hero, Howard Harvitz, is totally uncommitted as the story begins. He has put his plans to remarry his first wife on hold, he knows he is a hack as a free-lance writer, he considers himself a marginal Jew, and he has decided to visit Russia as an "intellectual" tourist (the kind who visits the Chekhov and Dostoevsky museums). His only recent act of commitment is a nominal one: he has changed his last name back from Harris to Harvitz. When he suddenly has responsibility thrust upon him, Harvitz will test the right to his true name.

Harvitz is approached by Levitansky, a Russian writer who is also a marginal Jew, and asked to smuggle Levitansky's stories out of the USSR. Levitansky has been denied publication in Russia, an act which puts both him and his work "in the drawer." Harvitz's cooperation might mean imprisonment for the American tourist who would prefer not to get involved. Such unwanted responsibility is the typical burden for Malamud's heroes. Harvitz has many good reasons for not risking his freedom for this stranger, but in the end he takes the chance. This heroic act pushes him to the center of all areas in which he was marginal. He is moved to commit himself after reading four of the stories, all of which show the small but terrifying suffering caused by one man's not taking responsibility for another. That the stories are Jewish in subject matter also influences Harvitz to aid a fellow Jew, and take responsibility for him, and helps Harvitz to earn the Jewish name he has already taken back. He also demonstrates the courage once part of the phrase "free lance" (of a knight errant) by risking his freedom for the work of a fellow writer, but most importantly, he demonstrates his commitment to mankind by getting involved in the life of a stranger.

This kind of courage is not always so easily forthcoming. Another margin dweller, Henry Levin, a floorwalker in the book department of Macy's, gives up his Jewish name and christens himself Henry Freeman. As Freeman, he falls in love with the aristocratic Lady of the Lake, and, believing that her questions about his religion are caused by her anti-Semitic prejudice, he denies that he is Jewish. To his chagrin, he discovers that she is a Buchenwald survivor, looking for someone to share her race's suffering and her own. Instead of freeing himself, Freeman only frees himself from his roots and his humanity. Instead of embracing his lady, he finds himself clutching a bloodless stone statue. The former book salesman finds himself in a land of imagination far beyond his own petty daydreams.

Freeman's lack of commitment is shared by Cronin in "A Choice of Profession" and Gans in "A Silver Crown." Both men are teachers, but are also men who are afraid of love. Both see commitment as something interesting to contemplate for the future, but both are afraid to give themselves entirely to a relationship. Cronin, who has just become a teacher, takes up with a woman whose past, he discovers, includes both incest and prostitution. Though he judges her entitled to her past mistakes, he not only gives her up, but he informs on her to a man he thinks has become her lover. Cronin, like most of Malamud's moral cowards, gives himself the best of motives for betraying the woman's trust. Though his real reason is jealousy, he convinces himself that he betrays her secret to protect her new lover, a family man. He also finds nothing wrong in setting himself up in judgment on the woman. He does feel some moral compunction and is uneasy enough about this incident to give up his newly chosen profession of teaching.

Gans, on the other hand, fails, even as he goes through the motions of total commitment. With his father dying of "cancer of the heart" and all medical alternatives exhausted, Gans sacrifices his rational principles and 986 dollars to buy a silver "healing crown" from a faith-healer. Though it would appear that Gans has done all he can to save his father, he has, in fact, done nothing more than buy off his guilt for not loving the old man. He questions the faith-healer minutely about the powers of the crown, but, as is usual in Malamud's short fiction, the answer is so simple that wise men overlook it (Gans is a high school biology teacher, but his name means "goose" or "fool"). The crown depends not on faith in it or in Judaism or even in God. Nothing else matters so long as Gans loves his father. When Gans admits he hates his father, the old man dies. In Malamud, even taking responsibility is not enough. It must be done without qualification, the moment a man looks for good reasons to do a good deed, the deed ceases to be good.

Two characters who ask no questions about love are Sobel, a shoemaker's apprentice in "The First Seven Years" and Finkle in "The Magic Barrel." In each case, they are faced by fathers who have idealistic expectations for marriage. Feld, the shoemaker, has dreams of an ideal match for his daughter and cannot believe that she would prefer his immigrant apprentice to a promising assimilated Jew. The choices for the daughter, like many in Malamud, are defined clearly between the material world and the spiritual. Her father's choice is a business student who reads only his texts, while Sobel reads for no other reason than to read. Feld cannot understand a man who reads when he has no desire to advance himself. After firing Sobel to get him away from his daughter, Feld suffers a heart attack (most illnesses, especially heart attacks and headaches, are more moral than medical in Malamud). When Sobel goes back to work for him, Feld realizes that the purity of his love has been refined in the suffering of the concentration camps and allows him to finish his seven-year apprenticeship in both the shop and in his daughter's heart.

Salzman, a *schadchen* ("marriage broker"), dreams of finding the perfect mate, not for his daughter, but for his customer Finkle. Finkle is a rabbinical student, and Salzman wants only the best for him. He claims to keep his files in a barrel whose magic assures happiness. Though the barrel and, in fact, his office are frauds, Salzman believes in the efficacy of his craft and is appalled when Finkle chooses Salzman's own daughter, who is a prostitute. Finkle, unlike Cronin in "A Choice of Profession," truly does not judge when he falls in love and comes fully alive when he offers flowers to Stella Salzman who is standing under a lamppost. Salzman, refusing to accept the magic of his own profession, chants the prayer for the dead signifying that the rabbinical student is lost to the faith. Almost certainly the reverse is true, by trusting in his love for another human being, Finkle has become ready to love God and man, and, therefore, will be worthy to be called rabbi at just the moment that Salzman stops thinking of him as a rabbi.

Sometimes the act of faith is a small gesture that points an uncommitted man toward commitment. In "A Summer's Reading," the hero claims falsely that he is not wasting his summer, but is spending it reading one hundred books. When a neighbor, Mr. Cattaranza, spreads the news of this virtuous act, the whole neighborhood begins to look on the boy as a hero. The boy brazens out his lie until Cattaranza discovers the lie, but does not betray him. This trust is enough to change the boy's life, and he finally sits down and begins to read. The same kind of faith is exhibited in "The German Refugee" where a refugee intellectual is encouraged by a young American student to give a lecture in English. The young man's faith in the refugee is enough to overcome his personal diffidence in his ability to handle English and the lecture succeeds. Such personal faith is not enough to sustain the refugee in a world gone mad, and he commits suicide by gassing himself after he learns that his gentile wife had converted and then had been murdered by the Nazis.

A more positive conclusion to this kind of exhibition of faith occurs in "Rembrandt's Hat" in which an art teacher, Arkin, casually mentions to a colleague, a failed sculptor named Rubin, that his hat looks like a hat Rembrandt was wearing in a self-portrait. Rubin takes this pleasantry for an insult, though Arkin cannot understand why. Eventually, the two men arrange their lives—from when they eat, to what exhibitions they visit, to their office hours—around the simple object of avoiding each other. It is not until Arkin takes the time to put himself in Rubin's place that he can see how the comparison with a great artist might humiliate one of little talent. When Arkin looks at slides of the Rembrandt portrait, he discovers that he was even wrong about what the hat looked like, making the original remark seem even more like a gratuitous insult. Though the point of contention is a small one, Arkin humbly admits his error, and this admission is enough to break down the wall that the two colleagues have built up. The center of this story is Arkin's compassion, the ability to put himself in another's place and to suffer with him. Compassion is the emotional act that compares to the intellectual act of commitment.

Compassion and commitment are not one-sided affairs. The mutuality of responsibility is seen in two stories, "Take Pity" and "Angel Levine," in which the recipients of mercy have trouble accepting the love proffered by another human being. In "Take Pity," Davidov, the recording Angel comes to Rosen to take account of his good deeds. Rosen tells how he tried to offer charity to a poor widow who, in her pride, kept refusing to accept it. Eventually, Rosen willed everything he owned to her and put his head in the oven and turned on the gas. When the anguished widow appears at the window looking in at the dead man, Rosen calls her a whore and closes the shade on her. Because she refused to take (accept) pity, Rosen has no deeds of charity to show the recording angel. Every act in Malamud is mutual in this way. There are always two people involved, and if either fails, both fail.

Manischevitz in "Angel Levine" also has trouble accepting proffered grace, but more out of despair than pride. He has grown so used to suffering that he cannot believe God cares about him or would send an angel to cure his sick wife. When the angel turns out to be a hip-talking Negro, Manischevitz believes even less, and yet, because it involves his wife, he is willing to go to Harlem to remove the last doubt that he is making a mistake. Though Levine dressed in a checked suit and pearl gray derby in Harlem looks even less like an angel than he did before, Manischevitz becomes convinced by the very absurdity of the situation that Levine must be what he says he is. Belief, after all, is accepting the impossible as true; it takes no faith to believe in the rational. When Manischevitz believes in Levine, that is, accepts the love that is offered him, the black angel literally earns his wings. Manischevitz returns home to find his wife is already up and cleaning the furniture. He regales her with the news that no reader of Malamud finds surprising, "there are Jews everywhere."

Though the bond between these two "men" is gentle, a number of the stories deal with the seemingly inescapable ties that join one human being with another. Often the bonds of hate or fear are just as powerful as those of love. The most straightforward demonstration of this is in "The Death of Me" where two tailor's assistants live only to torment each other. Their lives are defined and energized by a hatred whose origins are beyond reason. When the tailor separates the two so that they cannot expend their rage on each other, their productivity declines as does their interest in life itself. Only a return to the near-murderous rage stirs them back to life.

SHORT STORIES

Though "The Death of Me" goes no further than to establish this connection, several other stories examine its consequences. The "Talking Horse," Abramowitz, finds himself inextricably bound with his master, a mute clown named Goldberg. Though powerful enough to escape from Goldberg, Abramowitz stays, hoping to coax out of his master the secret of his own strange condition—what it is that gives him yearnings beyond those of an ordinary talking horse. Abramowitz puts up with endless abuse, but when he discovers that Goldberg has been lying to him, he goads his master into a tremendous struggle that makes Goldberg tear off Abramowitz's upper half, revealing him to be a centaur. Malamud makes it clear that without the struggle, Abramowitz would never know who he was and would be condemned to think of himself as a freak instead of a miracle. By working his character out through the struggle with another, Abramowitz is no longer trapped as a circus entertainer and is free to roam the prairies with the power of a beast and the intellect of a man.

Sometimes this link of hatred grows poisonous as in "The Bill" where Schlegel buys from the Panessa Grocery on credit and then comes to hate Panessa for trusting him. As his bill gets larger, Schlegel sees the grocer growing uglier until his stooped back seems to be hunched. Eventually this breach of trust grows so great that Panessa dies of it, and Schlegel, trying to say the right thing, finds that his "tongue hung in his mouth like dead fruit on a tree."

UNDERSTANDING BERNARD MALAMUD

The link of hate can also be redemptive as in "The Mourners," where a landlord grows to hate one of his obnoxious tenants to the point where his obsession is to get the man evicted from the building. When, at last, it seems the landlord has triumphed, he finds his tenant sitting *shiva* ("the formal act of mourning"). The landlord suddenly realizes that the mourning is for him, that his hatred has made him a dead man, and he covers his head and joins his tenant in mourning the inhumanity of the human race.

Most of Malamud's urban stories have the quality of still lives. The characters only occasionally go anywhere, they rarely move more than enough to survive, and they often end up in frozen attitudes like the mourners. Malamud's Italian stories, on the other hand, move at a much faster pace. The heroes of these stories, usually Jewish-Americans, are in a rush to get somewhere, but this haste gets entangled in a world of smouldering Italian passion and/or intrigue. The hero of "Behold the Key," an American student of Italian history, is led by his Italian guide on a wild goose chase in an effort to find an apartment. Ultimately the guide promises him one that was kept by a countess for her lover. After many comic disappointments and a few well-placed bribes, the apartment and its key are found, but when the apartment is opened all the furniture has been slashed by the spurned lover. In addition to jealousy, the lover's motive for vandalizing the apartment includes his hatred for the guide. Though the American has been a student of Italian history, this scene tells him more about the passionate spirit of the Italian people than all the books he has studied. The lover throws the key at the student leaving a permanent scar on his forehead. The student will be forever branded with this knowledge that comes from experience rather than study.

The same frenzied pace is found in the Fidelman stories ("Last Mohican," "Still Life," and "Naked Nude"). Malamud uses Fidelman to develop Henry James's favorite theme of the American innocent abroad, but in a most un-Jamesian manner. Fidelman is in constant motion as an array of charlatans, con men, obsessed women, and thieves test and change his American moral values. Fidelman keeps trying new kinds of art to relate to the Italians, but he is always one step behind. He also seeks, and occasionally participates in, a richness of passion not typical of Malamud's urban heroes.

Malamud's Italian stories cover thematically much the same ground as his urban Jewish ones, but the landscapes are much richer, filled with the antiquity of the country and the warmth of the Mediterranean skies. They tend to celebrate passion in a way that only a few of the urban stories do. "Life Is Better than Death" begins with the kind of mourning found in "The Mourners" or "The Bill," but ends with the heroine, a widow pregnant and deserted by a man she met in the cemetery, vowing never to mourn again. Though fully aware of death, she has committed herself to life.

BIBLIOGRAPHY

Primary Works

The Natural. New York: Harcourt, Brace, 1952.

The Assistant. New York: Farrar, Straus & Cudahy, 1957.

The Magic Barrel. New York: Farrar, Straus & Cudahy, 1958.

A New Life. New York: Farrar, Straus & Cudahy, 1961.

Idiots First. New York: Farrar, Straus, 1963.

The Fixer. New York: Farrar, Straus & Giroux, 1966.

A Malamud Reader. Ed. Philip Rahv. New York: Farrar, Straus & Giroux, 1967.

Pictures of Fidelman: An Exhibition. New York: Farrar, Straus & Giroux, 1969.

The Tenants. New York: Farrar, Straus & Giroux, 1971.

Rembrandt's Hat. New York: Farrar, Straus & Giroux, 1973.

Dubin's Lives. New York: Farrar, Straus & Giroux, 1979.

God's Grace. New York: Farrar, Straus & Giroux, 1982.

The Stories of Bernard Malamud. New York: Farrar, Straus & Giroux, 1983.

Critical Works

BIBLIOGRAPHY

Kosofsky, Rita. *Bernard Malamud: An Annotated Checklist.* Kent, Ohio: Kent State UP, 1970

Books

Astro, Richard, and Benson, Jackson, eds. *The Fiction of Bernard Malamud*. Corvallis: Oregon State University Press, 1977. This is a collection of original essays written for a symposium on Malamud at the school where he taught for a dozen years. Most of the contributors have written on Malamud before, but the

BIBLIOGRAPHY

collection provides a useful perspective on Malamud's
achievement through 1976. There is also a comprehensive
checklist of criticism on Malamud by Donald Risty.

Cohen, Sandy. *Bernard Malamud and the Trial by Love*.
Amsterdam: Editions Rodopi, N.V., 1974. Cohen discusses
Malamud's heroes in terms of eros and caritas, that is, selfish lust
and other-directed love of humanity. He creates a scale between
these two poles on which he measures Malamud's characters.

Ducharme, Robert. *Art and Idea in the Novels of Bernard
Malamud*. The Hague: Mouton, 1974. Ducharme sees Malamud's
heroes as idealists in their perceptions of love and freedom who
grow by tempering their idealism with a deeper understanding of
reality.

Field, Leslie A. and Field, Joyce, eds. *Bernard Malamud and the
Critics*. New York: New York University Press, 1970. A
comprehensive collection of essays embodying most of the
important criticism of Malamud to its date, the volume includes
21 essays.

Bernard Malamud: A Collection of Critical Essays. Englewood
Cliffs, N.J., Prentice-Hall, 1975. A second collection of essays by
the editors of the preceding item, this volume includes essays
written from 1970 to 1975.

Gunn, Giles B. "Bernard Malamud and the High Cost of Living."
Adversity and Grace: Studies in Recent American Literature.
Nathan A. Scott. Ed. U. of Chicago P, 1968. Gunn sees
Malamud's heroes as American innocents in the tradition of *The
Scarlet Letter*, *Billy Budd*, and *The Great Gatsby*. America is seen
as a land of promise betrayed where the hero tests his mettle, not
by success, but by failure. He argues that Malamud uses a
Whitmanesque technique of fusing opposites so that the

BIBLIOGRAPHY

sympathetic narrative voice balances the desperate conditions of
Malamud's heroes.

Hassan, Ihab. *Radical Innocence*. Princeton: Princeton UP, 1961.
161–68. Hassan shows how Malamud's irony balances the
affirmative tone of his novels. He sees Malamud's heroes as never
quite achieving the goals they set out to accomplish, and their
awkwardness in half-success as Malamud's statement of the
human condition.

Hershinow, Sheldon. *Bernard Malamud*. New York: Frederick
Ungar, 1980. Hershinow's survey of Malamud's output through
Dubin's Lives stresses his importance as a humanist and a
moralist and emphasizes his Old Testament antecedents,
particularly the Book of Job.

Richman, Sidney. *Bernard Malamud*. New York: Twayne, 1966.
Richman reviews Malamud's career to this point. He impressively
demonstrates Malamud's ability to balance ambiguities and
ironies so that the end result is positive. Richman explains
Malamud's debt to Dostoevsky in creating guilt-tormented
characters and his debt to Buber in developing his own
philosophy. He shows that the negative results of the heroes are
always balanced by an upward turn at the end, though this is
only a direction rather than an accomplishment.

Articles

Alter, Robert. "Malamud as Jewish Writer." *Commentary* 42. 3
(September 1966): 71–76. Alter argues that although Malamud
writes almost exclusively about Jews, there is no sense of a Jewish
community in his writing. In the process of writing about Jews,

BIBLIOGRAPHY

Malamud creates a new kind of folk legend that is mythical rather than sociological in nature.

Baumbach, Jonathan. "The Economy of Love: The Novels of Bernard Malamud." *Kenyon Review* 25 (1963): 438–57. Baumbach puts Malamud in the tradition of romance novelists like Cooper, Melville, and Hawthorne. He analyzes the use of seasonal motifs in the novels and finds Malamud's characteristic mode in the union of mythic ritual with everyday realism.

Bellman, Samuel. "Women, Children, and Idiots First: The Transformational Psychology of Bernard Malamud." *Critique* (1972–73): 123–38. Bellman argues that Malamud accomplishes the redemption of the lost by transforming their lives onto other levels of meaning. His approach shows how symbolic values work positively, even when the characters' everyday lives are tragic.

Desmond, John. "Malamud's Fixer: Jew, Christian, or Modern?" *Renascence* 27 (1975): 101–10. Desmond discusses Bok's discovery of his historical identity as a Jew, and then his modernity in recognizing the absence of God in our time. He sees Bok as more Christlike (especially in his compassion) than the Christians who torment him. Finally, he compares this existential Christ figure to the whole Christ, and finds him less truly loving because he yields to the same hatred perpetrated by his tormentors.

Friedberg, Maurice. "History and Imagination: Two Views of the Beiliss Case." *Midstream* 12 (Nov. 1966): 72–76. Friedberg discusses the historical incident behind *The Fixer*, the trial of Mendel Beiliss for the ritual murder of a Christian child in Kiev in 1913. Friedberg compares *The Fixer* to Maurice Samuel's *Blood*

BIBLIOGRAPHY

Accusation, a historical account of the Beiliss trial, and notes that Malamud's book, by concentrating on the victim, is less effective than Samuel's in presenting the historical forces arrayed against him.

Goldman, Mark. "Bernard Malamud's Comic Vision and the Theme of Identity." *Critique* 7 (1964–65): 92–109. Goldman argues that most of Malamud's work includes a comic view that requires the destruction of the hero's comic hubris. Once this mask of pride is fractured the hero can discover his true identity.

Goldsmith, Arnold. "Nature in Bernard Malamud's *The Assistant*." *Renascence* 29 (1977): 211–23. Goldsmith counters James Mellard's argument that the mythic value of Frank as restorer of the Wasteland can overcome the tragic tone of the novel. Goldsmith notes the importance of sea imagery as contrast to the pastoral and finds that the sense of drowning permeates the novel. He traces several image patterns, particularly those of the moon, of flowers, and of birds to show their primarily negative connotation.

Gollin, Rita. "Malamud's Dubin and the Morality of Desire." *Papers on Language and Literature* 18 (1982): 198–207. Gollin discusses the relation of romantic yearning to lust, showing how both can lead to failure as they become self-deceptive idealism or selfish possessiveness. She offers an extensive survey of these themes is Malamud's fiction and then goes on to demonstrate how Dubin finally chooses morality over the powerful urgings of desire.

Hays, Peter L. "The Complex Pattern of Redemption in *The Assistant*." *Centennial Review* 13 (1959): 200–214. Hays emphasizes the redemptive power of Morris's love which leads Frank from despair to hope. He argues that the mythic values of

BIBLIOGRAPHY

the novel, for example, Helen as fertility goddess, outweigh the ironic values stressed by many other critics. Hays discusses at length the influence of Jewish existential philosopher Martin Buber on the thinking of Malamud's Morris Bober.

Kennedy, Gerald J. "Parody as Exorcism: 'The Raven' and 'The Jewbird.'" *Genre* 13 (1980): 161–69. Kennedy sees "The Jewbird" as a parody of Poe's "The Raven." Both are works in which the hero tries to understand a mystic bird, and when he fails, tries to get rid of the bird. Kennedy also argues that the story marks Malamud's attempt to free his fiction from the gothicism and mysticism of his earlier works and that the Jewbird represents the Yiddish folk element in his fiction.

Lindberg-Seyersted, Brita. "A Reading of Bernard Malamud's *The Tenants*," *Journal of American Studies* 9 (Apr. 1975): 85–102. Lindberg-Seyersted emphasizes the importance of Lesser, the blundering hero-artist whose only passion is his art. She comments thoughtfully on the theme of the double in Malamud, particularly as it develops into the relation of master to novice. She analyzes the many literary allusions in the novel and shows how Malamud creates a surrealistic mood through the manipulation of tense, the use of dreams, and the movement in and out of the fiction written by the two tenants.

Malin, Irving. "Portrait of the Artist in Slapstick: Malamud's *Pictures of Fidelman*." *Literary Review* 24 (1980): 121–38. Malin analyzes the different styles employed by Fidelman as an artist and Malamud as a portrayer of Fidelman. He shows how Fidelman grows by surrendering to his "deep longings" in both art and love. He also convincingly demonstrates the way Malamud uses the comic tone of the novel to support Fidelman through his small disasters.

BIBLIOGRAPHY

Mandel, Ruth. "Bernard Malamud's *The Assistant* and *A New Life*: Ironic Affirmation." *Critique* 7.2 (1964–65): 110–21. Mandel sees all sacrifice in these novels as basically selfish, thereby undercutting the value of whatever affirmation appears to be made. She argues that the suffering so essential to Malamud's characters is useless since it leads only to more suffering.

Mellard, James. "Malamud's Novel's: Four Versions of Pastoral." *Critique* 9.2 (1967): 5–19. Mellard argues that Malamud's first four novels are versions of the pastoral myth which finds its source in the story of Perceval and the Wasteland. He emphasizes the symbolic use of the cycle of the seasons in each novel and does a good job of explaining father/son relationships (often surrogate ones) as they parallel such relationships in the myth.

Rovit, Earl. "Bernard Malamud and the Jewish Literary Tradition." *Critique* 3 (1960). Rovit analyzes the influence of Yiddish folktales on Malamud's work. He points out the pluses and minuses of Malamud's obvious concern with craft as opposed to the artlessness of the originals.

Siegel, Ben. "Victims in Motion: Bernard Malamud's Sad and Bitter Clowns." *Northwest Review* 5 (1962): 69–80. In a largely negative review of Malamud's early novels, Siegel finds Malamud writing ideas rather than creating characters, describing motives rather than explaining them, and being ingenious rather than insightful. Siegel has little patience with Malamud's symbolism, pathos, and irony, and prefers the more realistic novels like *A New Life*.

Wasserman, Earl R. "*The Natural*: Malamud's World Ceres." *Centennial Review* 9 (1965): 438–60. Wasserman has produced a most sophisticated Jungian reading of *The Natural*, showing how the Perceval story is built on even more primal archetypes, particularly that of the Magna Mater, the fertile Earth Mother.

BIBLIOGRAPHY

The punning title of the article suggests Wasserman's interest in the names and puns of the novel.

Wegelin, Christof. "The American Schlemiehl Abroad: Malamud's Italian Stories and the End of American Innocence." *Twentieth Century Literature* 19 (Apr. 1973): 77–88. Wegelin relates Malamud to James and Hawthorne, focusing particularly on James's Christopher Newman and the theme of American innocence in the face of European worldliness. He examines the attempts of the Americans to find spiritual liberation and shows how this fails in the ironically named Henry Freeman in "Lady of the Lake," but succeeds after many trials with Fidelman. He also notes that by the end of the novel, Fidelman loses all sense of moral superiority found in the American heroes abroad of James and Howells.

Interviews

Shenker, Israel. "Bernard Malamud on Writing Fiction." *Writer's Digest*, July 1972: 22–23.

Tyler, Ralph. "A Talk with the Novelist." *New York Times Book Review*, 18 February 1979, p. 1.

INDEX

INDEX

INDEX

INDEX

INDEX